Peggy Harris

LIFE ON A
DARTMOOR SCRAPYARD

The later years

Peggy Harris

LIFE ON A
DARTMOOR SCRAPYARD

The later years

FOREWORD BY CHRIS CHAPMAN

A SKERRYVORE PRODUCTION

In fond memory of Mr Small (Reece Morgan)

First published 2014
A Skerryvore Production
Southernhay, North Street, South Molton, Devon EX36 3AN
Tel & Fax: 01647 231508

Photographs, unless acknowledged otherwise
© Chris Chapman www.chrischapmanphotography.co.uk

Edited by Sue Viccars
Designed by Emily Kingston

British Library Cataloguing in Publication Date
A catalogue record for this book is available from the British Library

ISBN 978-0-9931039-1-9

Typesetting and origination by Blackingstone Publishing
Printed in Great Britain

Front cover Peggy Harris driving a restored Ferguson T20 © Chris Chapman 2013
Page 2 Peggy doing logs on Dartmoor in 2013
Back cover Jed Chapman and Peggy ferreting in the snow

CONTENTS

Peggy and her daughter Clare in 1989

FOREWORD

It is nearly ten years since Peggy Harris first brought her writings to our house, and five years since the publication of *Life on a Dartmoor Scrapyard: The early years*. Since then we have got to know Peggy really well, and without wanting to cause her embarrassment she is now considered part of the family. It's always a pleasure to see her. Often she will turn up bearing gifts, a tin of Quality Street for Jed, a plant for Helen, a useful bit of scrap or a tool for me, a delicious cake for teatime. For a couple of years we had the loan of a mini tractor and trailer she had fashioned for her daughter Clare when she was younger, and in turn our son Jed took great pleasure in driving this up and down the field collecting sticks for the fire.

We have had numerous conversations about life on Dartmoor (especially when waiting for the elusive Benson to appear, as you will learn on reading this book!) and I realised early on that Peggy's natural gift for storytelling was because she was honest and always spoke from the heart. Most of her stories told in our kitchen made us laugh, but on odd days she would turn up tired and upset and in need of a sympathetic ear. If she thought someone was simply out for themselves and was trying to take advantage of her, or had committed a misdemeanour, she showed no hesitation in venting her anger, often in colourful language. We became used to this and as her frustration wasn't aimed at us we were happy to listen and sometimes give advice. It was through these outpourings that we gained an insight into how life had treated her in the past, and was continuing to treat her.

A couple of years ago I suggested she write a second book based on what had happened to her just before and after Sam died. She said that she might do it, but in her own time. Months passed by and then suddenly she found focus and disappeared to her daughter's in Herefordshire and put some stories together. When she came back she gave them to Helen and me to read. We were greatly moved by these new stories. They spoke of events that one wished didn't happen but through the telling they brought about compassion and showed just how strong Peggy has had to be. There is a toughness of spirit in her that takes on what is thrown at her and somehow overcomes. It is an admirable trait and one that I have come across before in country people who have had to live life hard.

But as well as being warm-hearted I've also learnt over the years just how incredibly capable Peggy is, often putting me to shame! We've done hedging together, fencing, woodcutting and numerous jobs that come with owning land. She is blessed with the strength of an ox, and as I get older and show my frustration at not being able to do what I could in my twenties, she wades in, pushes me aside and takes over. But she never scolds or ridicules; she just gets on with it in the same way that she just gets on with life. For my part she has taught me a great deal, and strengthened my faith in that most people are decent and wish to live nobly.

Dartmoor is a harsh landscape and yet has its own special beauty. It is where Peggy, who certainly is noble, truly belongs.

Chris Chapman
Throwleigh, Dartmoor
October, 2014

INTRODUCTION

After the publication of my first book, *Life on a Dartmoor Scrapyard: The early years*, readers have been asking me about what happened next in my life. For years I kept this secret because I have been too embarrassed and, at times, ashamed. Now that I am feeling more confident, rather than looking for sympathy, I want to show that it is possible to overcome obstacles in life, no matter how hurtful they may be.

Writing this second book has been the hardest thing I have ever had to do. I am now 48 years old and it may surprise some people that I am still working part-time in a scrapyard! On other days I help old ladies with their housework and gardens and, in my spare time, help a friend with various jobs, putting up fencing and restoring his tractors.

For years I lived in fear that my ex-partner and the father of my daughter would find me. I struggled with the injuries that he caused and bouts of depression, but despite it all I was still determined to have some sort of life. It was a bad hand of cards that I was dealt, but I wanted to make sure my daughter didn't turn out like me. I wanted her to grow up like a lady, and I'm pleased to say that she has.

My second book tells some of the stories of the people and the acts of kindness which have helped me get to where I am today.

Sam (driving) and Bob leading their ponies down to Lettaford

THE EARLY YEARS

I thought we'd managed to publish all my childhood memories in my first book, but I keep recalling people who came looking for car parts, funny incidents, the scrapes us kids got into, the animals we looked after... so here's a further collection of scrapyard stories.

SWORE AT MOTHER

I must have only been about five. Some customers used to come up to the yard and if I went to see what they were up to or if I irritated them somehow, they sometimes swore at me. So I learnt to swear at a young age.

One Saturday evening Father had picked up a lorry load of jumble that was left over from a local jumble sale. My brothers Jim and Bob and I were dressing up. I had pulled on a pair of golf shoes that were ten sizes too big for me. I was still wearing my wellies on the inside. It must have been getting on as Mother came out and said it was time for bed. We were having fun on the back of the lorry with Father leaning over the tailboard. He was poking through the boxes of china. We took no notice of her and didn't go in. Mother shouted for us to get off the lorry and to come in for bed. I was annoyed and swore at her. She was nearly up and over the side board in a flash. I saw her coming and realised I was in for it. I climbed out over the opposite side of the lorry and started to run down the lane as I knew what was coming. I didn't have time to kick off the big shoes. It was hard to run; it was like having clown feet. Mother caught me and thrust me headfirst between her knees and walloped my arse – it glowed all night.

FERTILISER SACK

Several people have come up to me and said, 'Cor! I remember you when you was a little maid. I remember you running round in a fertiliser sack.' I said, 'Well, it must have been raining.'

I remember cutting a hole in the bottom of a bag for my head to go through and a slit for each of my arms to come out off, the bag hanging down past my knees. At least it kept me dry. You couldn't do it today because they don't have hundredweight fertiliser sacks any more. I imagine it was a blue sack with ICI written on it.

HEDGEHOG

My twin brother Bob reminded me that when we were really young in the early 1970s we had gone with Father up to Whiddon Down to Mark Small's to buy scrap.

Mark was a gypsy and Father was great friends with him. They struck a good number of deals together over the years and spent many happy hours in the pub afterwards.

On arriving I found a hedgehog in his field. Father was one for a joke and so he encouraged me and Bob to go and put it in Mark's bed. The next time he saw Sam he told him that he had found a hedgehog in his bed. 'It wasn't the prickles that got me, it was the bloody fleas!'

INDIGNANT

An old teacher of mine told me that when I was about six I would walk around the playground with her at lunchtime. She said it was a Monday and she had asked me if I'd had a good weekend. I told her it had been a bad weekend as my grandfather had hurt his back. She had asked me if he was all right. I looked up at her very indignant and said, 'He's not all right, he's Alfred Baker.' I hadn't come across the word before and thought it was a name.

TRIP TO THE BEACH

Sue Price was a teacher at Chagford Primary School when I was seven. I stayed in her class for two years. In one of her lessons she was talking about the seaside and she asked who had been. All the children in the class apart from me had been to the seaside. She was very surprised to hear I hadn't even seen the sea or a beach before, so one Saturday she invited me to go. I was very excited. Mother made me wear a cotton dress with flowers on it, which I didn't want to wear but Mother told me I had to look smart. Mrs Price brought her mother along as well. I don't really remember playing in the sand or sea but I remember going!

Mrs Price told me that my Father had told us to keep away from the VAT office as we passed through Exeter as it wasn't a good place to go.

One day when I was 13 and at secondary school I missed the bus. Mrs McGlyn took me back to her house and her husband rang

Father to come and meet us. Father said I was to walk home on my own as he wasn't coming to meet me. So Mr McGlyn gave me a lift to the top of our road. He said he had to leave me to walk the rest of the way home down the lane on my own as the snow was blowing and it was dark – he had to leave me to find my own way home. I think he felt sorry for me.

BANDAGING DONKEY JACK

One Christmas I was given a set of pony bandages by the Ardens. We had been learning to bandage tails and legs at Pony Club, so I decided to practise on Donkey Jack.

In the winter Donkey Jack used to come in at night as it was cold. I would go sit with him and hang an oil lantern on a small nail. It was a small stable which Mother had made it for him. It was about six foot square and in the corner was a small hay rack. While he was munching his hay I would bandage up his legs. He looked real smart with bright red bandages on. He didn't have much of a tail, but when I wrapped the bandage around the full length it was all red and looked a little silly with a few hairs sticking out the bottom.

BROKE DOWN AND HAD TO SLEEP IN THE VAN

Mother, Father and I had gone out to Bow one evening to see a customer. Father had bought a vanload of scrap off him, and loaded it. They sat and talked late into the evening, and it must have been nearly midnight when we left. Mother was driving and Father was nodding off. I was very tired and had school the next day. We always drove the back road through the narrow lanes from Bow, through Spreyton, then up to Whiddon Down.

This evening we hadn't quite got to Spreyton and were heading up a slight hill. Mother was changing gear as we had a heavy load on. All of a sudden the van stopped. Mother tried the engine several times and it wouldn't start – it was pitch black outside and a long way from a phone box. The nearest one was back at Bow or further on at Spreyton. The decision was made to go to sleep until daylight.

Well, Father had no problem going to sleep. He dropped off in a minute, snoring loudly. Mother leaned over the steering wheel, and it wasn't long before she too was breathing deeply, with a softer snore. I was sat between them in the pitch black. It was still warm in the cab from the engine. It felt like an age sat in the dark. I could feel the warm air changing to cold but I must have dropped off as

I woke up with a stiff neck. It was just breaking daylight and Mother was stirring. Father awoke and suggested that we walk back to Bow and get the chap we'd bought the scrap off to help us. So Mother and I started walking back down the road. The further we walked the lighter it got. We met a milkman and told him we had broken down and that Father was waiting up the road in the van. We bought a bottle of milk off him and shared it as we walked back to Bow.

When we arrived at the customer's house it was very quiet; everyone was still asleep. We banged loudly on the door, and it felt like an age before anyone answered. Eventually the chap got up and made us tea and toast. Then we jumped in his van and he took us back to Father. He was having a hot cup of tea with the milkman, who'd gone home and made a flask.

We all looked on as the customer tried to start the van but there was no joy, so he hitched us to the back of his van and slowly towed us back to the scrapyard. I missed school, and my brothers hadn't got up to go either.

I GOT SHOT

Mark Philips used to come over to the scrapyard on Saturdays, and Father would pay him to clean metals and to do odd jobs through the holidays. He was a little younger than me and would come over to play with us kids. When growing up we have all played silly games. Well, I would play dangerous games. We would drive old cars up and down the lane and around the field. One game was to play with an air pistol and an air rifle. We had been watching the television programme *The Professionals*, where they would jump and roll over cars. We had this game where we would run round and jump on and off cars, sliding down the bonnet. We would shoot near each other but we would shoot so as not to hit anyone else. The air guns had weak springs. The only rules were to shoot close, but not to hit anyone. We would hide and jump out on each other, then run and hide again.

One day while playing the game I slipped and fell to the ground. I had winded myself and I was lying still when Mark arrived. He stood above me. I looked up and he took aim and fired. I couldn't believe it! He had only just shot me in the head, behind my right ear, and the bugger was loading again for another go. This wasn't part of the game. I know the guns had weak springs but up close it hurt. The lead pellet was stuck in my

14

head. I jumped up and grabbed the gun off him. 'You shouldn't shoot me in the head!' I screamed.

I couldn't go to Mother and ask her to pull the pellet out of my head because I didn't want a telling off from her for playing a dangerous game. So I cleaned myself up and went over to my Nan's across the field, as their farm was on the same footpath as our place. I got there in the late afternoon and sat and had tea with them. While Aunty Angel was washing up the dishes I finally built up the courage to ask her to pick out the pellet. I made her promise not to tell Mother before I'd told her what had happened. Aunty Angel was furious. She told me it was a dangerous game. I explained to her that Mark had shot me when I had fallen down and that he wasn't supposed to.

Mark used to have to walk along the footpath past my Nan's farm on his way home. Aunty Angel said she gave him a right telling off when he passed through a few days later.

Peggy's mother Doreen was born at Park Gate near Southampton on 26 July 1926, and came to Dartmoor when she was 19

CANDLE MAKING

When the boys shared a caravan with Father they used to melt candle wax to make a new candle. One afternoon I said to Father, 'I could make some candles' as I had watched Jim several times. We had a tin cone that was used in a bakery to make cream horns. We would drop a piece of string down through the point for a wick, and melt the cold candle wax in a saucepan on a small gas cooker that was in the caravan. When the wax was melted we would pour it gently into the tin cone, holding the string in the middle.

Anyway, it looked easy. I had all the cones threaded and was waiting for the wax to melt but I had got it too hot – the pan caught on fire. I pulled it off the stove but the saucepan fell to the floor and landed on a pouffe. It was all a blaze of fire. I rushed to open the door and kicked the flaming pouffe out. I was so lucky. I could have burnt the whole caravan and then where would Father and the boys have slept – under the stars?

COLIN

Colin was a little tike who loved football and he used to drive me mad trying to get me to play. So one day I told him if he could score 100 goals I would keep the football. I saved a few but I let them pass. It took ages. I kept the ball and he walked off home quite happy. Later that evening his mother rang and asked if he could have it back as he was rather upset. I gave it back to him the next day.

One summer he fell out with his mother and came down our place dragging his sleeping bag. He said to Mother that he had fallen out with his mother and that he was moving in with us. So he stayed for a few days with Bob and Jim. He was about eight.

When he grew into his teens he would bum fags off Father. I decided to put him off fags so I soaked the baccy in diesel and rolled it for him, but that didn't stop him! I dried dock leaves and made him a fag out of that, but that didn't work either. He didn't know I was cooking up bad fags until one day I filled one with three or four red-head matchsticks. When he had smoked to about halfway it exploded into flames and nearly burnt his nose, but even that didn't put him off! He still bummed fags off Father.

FRED NORTHWAY

When we lived at the scrapyard there was an old man around called Fred Northway. He used to walk around the fields looking at Molly Croft's ponies. He often came out the top gate just above our place. You always knew when he'd been around, as you could smell his pipe. He was a slim-built man, often wearing a long overcoat and welly boots. He wore glasses and a trilby hat. He would be heading up to Lettaford and he would stop in and have a chat with Old Fred on the corner, and then he often called in to see Chris and

Matty Hill at Lettaford Farm. I loved to have a chat with him; he would make his pipe squeak by sucking on it and it sounded like a frightened rabbit. So of course when you saw him you would always ask him to make his pipe squeak.

Sometimes in the evening coming home in the van you would find Fred leaning in the hedge to let you pass. He would make us jump because the only way we knew he was there was when the headlights would just catch his glasses. Father would shout out to him, ''Night, Fred,' or sometimes pull up for a chat.

MOTHER AND HERBS

If anyone had a cold – or the first sign of one – Mother would put blackcurrant leaves in the teapot. If you already had a cold you didn't notice the smell, but if you didn't you could smell it. She would lace the pot with allsorts. When Father had a bad chest, she would make him a dish with bread, hot water, an Oxo cube and yarrow, then send him to bed to sweat it out. Father swore by it.

Mother treated me for boils once. She picked ragwort flowers and wrapped them in tissues and placed it on the boil. The flowers drew the pus out and over the next few days – she had to change the dressing several times – it began to clear the boil up. I've never had one since.

DRAGGED ACROSS DARTMOOR

One summer I stayed with the Ardens, our neighbours at Stiniel, and rode a chestnut pony there called Michaelmas. He was a very young green pony that hadn't been broken in for very long. A young girl was working there at the time, I forget her name. Johnny Arden told her to ride out with me. I saw a car parked in the drive so I suggested that we rode down the back lane. She said that he'd be OK, and that we should go out the front entrance. She lead the way past the car but I felt Michaelmas back up. He was looking at the car, which was a blue Austin Maxi. We got safely past it but then all of a sudden he started to buck and kicked the front of the car, dropping me on the road. I landed hard on my hip and he charged off up the road, bucking and kicking. The young girl tried to catch him, but he jumped a five-bar gate. I was in agony.

Johnny and the owner of the car picked me up and helped me walk into the house. Johnny's mother-in-law made me a cup of sweet tea. You could nearly stand the spoon up in it; she told me the sugar was good for shock. Johnny saddled up his horse and charged around the farm trying to catch Michaelmas. He was gone for some time. I was worried I might have broken something, but if I had I wouldn't have been able to stand or walk. The pain – I'd never felt anything like it.

Johnny arrived back in the yard with one very hot steaming pony (his own horse was just as hot). He shouted to me to come out and ride the pony as he was going to lead me out on him. I climbed aboard and we left the yard at a trot and went for a two-and-a-half-hour ride. I had to grin and bear the pain. The next morning I could hardly walk. The pain was unbearable, so I asked if I could go to the doctor (which was unusual for me). So his mother-in-law took me to see the doctor, who told me I had probably bruised the bone and that I should keep moving so that the muscle would free up. Johnny had me walking everywhere. It took me weeks to get over that fall.

I didn't ride Michaelmas for some time. Then one day Liz Arden said she was going to take me out on Michaelmas, so she led me on a plough line (a long rope). The pony was going well, so we rode out to Tawton Gate and up over the moor. He was going so well that Liz handed me the plough line. We trotted over the moor and came to a river, and Michaelmas wanted to stop for a drink. Liz rode up the slope; I pulled Michaelmas up and trotted up to join her. As I got up beside Liz, without warning Michaelmas put in an almighty buck that somersaulted me into the air over his head. As I landed he galloped off, but I still had the plough line, so I grabbed hold with both hands. Before I knew it I was being dragged across the moor on my belly. It was like grass surfing. I could hear Liz shouting 'Don't let go!' I was hanging on, but he wasn't slowing down. He was heading down towards the road because on the other side were some wild ponies. I avoided a few rocks but I was being dragged into a rocky area. I thought to myself, bugger this, I'm not going to eat granite – so I let go.

We caught him after he had stopped and settled with the wild ponies, pulling him in on the plough line. We remounted and finished the ride.

Peggy holding Jack at Tedburn St Mary Show in 2002

TOWING HOME OLD CARS

I steered towed cars home from the age of 13. We used a tow bar, which is a straight iron bar with Ds on the end; these are iron loops with a bolt going through them that are attached to each vehicle, so you couldn't go far.

The second car I ever towed home was an old Vauxhall out at South Zeal, several miles through the country lanes. When Father and I arrived around the back of some garages, I saw the Vauxhall parked up next to the hedge.

'There it is,' said Father. I got out of the Transit van and walked over to the pale blue Vauxhall. I peered in through the dusty window. There weren't any seats, so how was I going to steer that? It was an empty shell. I turned round to Father and said, 'There's no seats Dad, where am I going to sit?' 'We'll get an old orange box for you,' he said.

At that moment the owner came walking down the path from his house. He and Father were soon in deep conversation. They opened the garage door and started to load up the Transit with old scrap. When they'd almost finished, Father asked, 'You haven't got an old orange box for the maid to sit on?' indicating towards me. 'Yeah Sam,' he replied, disappearing back towards the house. After a while he came back with an orange box tucked underneath his arm. Handing it to me he smiled. 'There you go maid, you ride home on that.'

19

We hitched up the car onto the back of the van. I set my seat close to the steering wheel. The man walked up to Father, said a few words and then we were off: with a jerk and a bang the wheels started rolling. All I could see was the backlights of the van in front of me.

It wasn't long before we came to a junction and had to stop. My box flew right up underneath the steering wheel, then with another jerk and a bang, jerk, jerk we were off again, but my box had shot back to the back of the vehicle. It was like this all the way home. Every junction or every time we had to stop my box would fly out from underneath me. I was glad when we got home.

The next hair-raising ride home was with Bob, my twin brother, in the early nineties. When I was visiting him one day he told me he had several cars to pick up from a farm four miles away near Chagford. He wanted to know if I would help him out by towing home two cars as he had five to pick up. 'OK,' I said, and off we set.

Out and around Chagford all the lanes are very narrow. Bob was driving a Transit pickup, and the hedges clipped the wing mirrors on both sides as we drove along. When we arrived there, Bob had to back down a narrow drive into a yard. There were four old Minis and one old Peugeot parked up on the grass.

The owner, a retired contractor, came out and had a chat with Bob and asked him which ones he wanted first. Bob said that we'd take two Minis 'load one, tow one'. The old chap said he would load one with his tractor. We weren't there long; they loaded a Mini on the back of the truck and hitched one up on the tow bar. We were ready to go and said our 'cheerios', and told him we'd be back later for the others. Bob said, 'If you have any problems, shout out of your windows and I'll stop, OK?' 'OK,' I replied.

Off we set. The truck roared as it pulled up the steep drive into the narrow lanes – around the corner, through a little hamlet of four houses and a small farm, then up the hill. Everything was running smoothly, and then all of a sudden I heard a strange wobbly noise coming from the back. I felt the back wheel fall off, and the back corner dropped down with a bump onto the brake drum. There was a very loud scratching and grinding as the bottom of the Mini scraped along the tarmac, and it echoed throughout the car.

This was a very early Mini with sliding windows; it took me ages to get the window open. All I could see was the back end of a minivan and the backlights of Bob's truck. Every time I went to shout out of the window, a bramble or a stinging nettle would swipe me. He wouldn't have heard me anyway as the truck was roaring along. I tried pumping the brakes and they didn't work. I then pulled the handbrake and that got his attention.

He pulled up and came back to see what was wrong. He didn't need to ask – he could see for himself. When I got out and looked down the road I could see a white line marking where we had come. We had to take a wheel off the Mini on the truck. Bob lifted up the back corner and held it while I put the wheel on, as we had no jack. Eventually we got home. 'We'll pick the wheel up on our way back for the next two cars,' Bob told me. We never found it, but you could see how far he had towed me with the missing wheel.

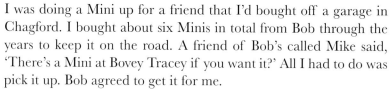

I was doing a Mini up for a friend that I'd bought off a garage in Chagford. I bought about six Minis in total from Bob through the years to keep it on the road. A friend of Bob's called Mike said, 'There's a Mini at Bovey Tracey if you want it?' All I had to do was pick it up. Bob agreed to get it for me.

It was a cold frosty day in the middle of February when we arrived. I could see it parked up on the side of the road; it was orange but it had no windscreen. We hitched it up and set off home. It was so cold my hands were nearly frozen to the steering wheel. It started to sleet. As I was pulled along the sleet blew in and stuck to me. I wouldn't recommend it to anyone; I was nearly blue when I got home.

THE BLIND BOY PAUL

Paul and Colin Harvey were two boys who lived at Lettaford. They would come down at weekends. Paul was a few years younger than me and Bob and he was partially sighted, but that never held him back. He would find his way around the scrapyard unaided. He loved cars. He would get us to take out speedos (speedometers) because they were different shapes and he would hold them up to the light as he liked to see the colours through the indicator, oil and ignition lights. His mother must have had a shed full.

BERT

Bert was a tubby little old man from Whiddon Down. He often came to the scrapyard for bits of iron as he was always making and mending things for different people in the area. He would pick up lawn mower engines as he tinkled with them as well. Poor old Bert would dribble as he talked to you.

Father used to get me to help carry his pieces of iron and put them into his white Reliant three wheeler. As I got older Bert became a bit saucy with me. He would say all sorts of funny things to me like 'many a tune played on an old fiddle'. I would just laugh as I didn't know what he was on about. I was about fourteen and only learnt in later life what he meant.

One day I wanted to use Jim's generator to charge a battery. Jim was away for the weekend. As I pulled the engine over and started it the pull start rope came out in my hand. I charged the battery, but as Mother was going to Okehampton I loaded the generator in the back of the lorry and hopped in with her. When we got to Whiddon Down we found Bert in his workshop. I asked him if he would fix Jim's generator? He said he would and I could pick it up later. Mother and I called in on the way back home and he had fixed it. I asked him how much it would cost me? He said, 'A kiss or £5.' I gave him a fiver: I wasn't going to kiss him!

Bert used to be a farrier in his working days. He said he was going to get some tools together and teach me to shoe (I had a pony at the time). First lesson he showed me how to trim the hoofs. He had made a front set of shoes in his workshop, and said he would talk me through how to put the shoes on. As I bent over holding the pony's hoof between my knees, Bert started to touch me on my backside. I put the hoof down and stood up and looked at him hard. Bert wiped his mouth with the back of his hand, saying, 'Come on, you'll never get the shoes on like this.' Gesturing with the hammer I replied, 'Touch me again and you'll know it.'

That was the first and last set of shoes I put on. I decided it wasn't worth learning.

PENSION BOOK

When I was in my early teens I use to go to Newton Abbot in the holidays to buy chickens from the market. Sometimes I would catch the market bus down from Beetor Cross or I would get a lift with Mother when she was going to Gorman's scrapyard with a load of metal.

I would buy hens and old cockerels, the hens for laying eggs and the cockerels for Father to kill for dinner. Sometimes I would buy a hen and chicks and I would sell the young hen birds at point-of-lay to anyone who was interested when they came to the yard. There was a man from Chagford, an Irishman called John Sheridan. He often came to the yard for parts for his Morris 1000 van and to have a look around. He was interested in the young hens I had, and so he bought them.

A month went by and he came up one evening and asked me for the pension book for the birds. Of course he was winding me up. He said, 'The hens must be old because they have no teeth!' I chased him out into the yard – bloody fool!

TESSA

We had all sorts of creatures come through the scrapyard, from pigs and goats to ponies and donkeys, even peacocks.

One day this chap turned up with a vanload of scrap and in the front seat was a small terrier. He said to me, 'Do you want a dog?' I had a good look at her and she seemed a friendly little thing. She had short hair, a ginger head and a white body, which was very wriggly and pleased to see me. I said I would take her.

He said, 'She's a good little dog but she's in pup.' I took her and called her Tessa. She stuck to me like glue. She came everywhere I went in the truck. When she had her puppies she only had two. This was a good thing because it was only two homes to find. I'd already found a home for one before they were born, and a customer took a liking to the other one.

Tessa was a sweet little thing. She liked to ride on my motorbike. Every time I started it up, she would rush out and jump up onto the tank. She would stand there while I rode up and down the lane, but if I rode on the road I would put her inside my coat. She would poke her head out and the tops of her ears would blow in the wind. When I talked to her I could feel her tail wagging inside my coat.

One day I took her to a dog show and she won the 'Dog with the Waggiest Tail' class, and the 'Best Trick', which was of course riding on a motorbike, which caused a good laugh.

We had other dogs at the time. There was Patsy, a Springer

spaniel, Tike, a lurcher and Jim's terrier, Lucky. Tike and Patsy were chained up and let off several times a day, but you had to keep an eye on them, as they would take themselves off hunting rabbits. The whole lot would go and they'd be away for hours. When they came back they would be covered in mud. The worst thing Tessa would do was roll in sheep shit. She would come back green and stinking.

If I wouldn't get up in the morning, Mother would send Tessa in. She knew that she would try to get in under the covers and this would make me move like lightning. Tessa had another brood of pups, five this time, and Mother kept one because Jim had lost Lucky. I found homes for the other four.

Time went on, and I had Tessa for several years. There was a woman who would come up to the yard most weeks with her son looking for spare parts. She always asked if she could have Tessa as she thought she was beautiful. I would always say, 'No, you can't have her, she's not for sale.' She would spend all the time waiting for her son, fussing Tessa. I was sometimes worried that she might just take her. I was pregnant with my daughter Clare at the time and I gave up work a couple of days before I gave birth. I left Tessa with my father to look after while I had Clare, and came back to the yard after five days in hospital. Tessa was gone. I said to Father, 'Where's Tessa?' 'Oh, I gave her away to that woman who wanted her.' I said that she was my dog and I didn't want her to be given away, especially to her. He said, 'You don't want a dog now, you've got a baby.' That woman never ever came back to the yard and I never saw Tessa again.

LIFTING CARS AND ENGINES

Growing up on a scrapyard I became very strong. I was stronger than I realised. I thought nothing of lifting up cars by their wheel arches to remove the wheels. One day two brothers who were in their late fifties came from Hatherleigh. They used to be regular customers. They wanted a couple of wheels and tyres off a car but they didn't have a jack. I told them to undo the wheel nuts and I would lift the car up for them so they could remove the wheels. I was in my late teens then, and didn't see them again for some years.

Years later I was up visiting Bob, when these two brothers arrived;

now in their late sixties, they were looking a lot older and greyer. They were reminiscing about the old days when Father was alive. They both turned to me and one said, 'The last time I saw you – you were picking up cars by their wheel arches,' and the other, 'Cor yeah, if you'd asked £20 a wheel I wouldn't have argued with you!'

One time in my early teens Mother and I had been sent to South Zeal to collect ten engines from the council house estate. We had to pick these engines up from a bloke's garage; Father said that he'd help us load them.

We arrived and found the man waiting for us. I thought to myself, 'Good, an extra pair of hands, we'll soon load these engines.' I helped Mother back up to the door. The engines varied in sizes and the bloke then told us he had a bad back and couldn't help, so it was down to Mother and me to load them. The big engine we could hardly lift high enough to slide in the back of the van, so we decided to load all the smaller engines first. As we put more engines in the back, the lower the tail of the van was going down. When we came to the real heavy ones, it wasn't so high to lift them. The man just kept saying, 'Sorry I can't help, I have a bad back!' We were two females, and Mother was in her mid-fifties – he just made himself look stupid.

Peggy and her friend Roy repairing a clutch on a Ferguson T20

TUBBY BRAILEY

Alan Brailey from Bovey Tracey was known to us as Tubby. I don't why as he wasn't a short, fat man – but we always knew him as Tubby. He used to work repairing stone walls and bridges, but he had a heart problem and retired early. He was a happy-go-lucky, pleasant man. When we were young he used to come up every weekend with his father-in-law Mr Harvey looking for parts, things he could make a deal on. He often bought Triumph cars from us.

Mr Harvey was a very nice old man. In the winter he would wear a trilby and in the summer a straw hat. He nearly always arrived with a wicker basket full of vegetables – beans, apples, carrots – he was a very keen gardener. He always found time to talk to us kids.

As time went on Tubby began to come up without him, and it was only in the later years that I realised that he must have passed on. On a Saturday Tubby would often give me a lift over to the Ardens so I could go riding if I couldn't get one from anyone else. He was very generous like that and would go out of his way.

He was one of Father's pall bearers at the funeral in 1988 but continued to go up to the yard. After Father had died Bob was left running the yard. Bob has always been a bit of a practical joker, and poor old Tubby fell for one of Bob's pranks. Bob had jacked a car up and placed a false pair of booted legs poking out from underneath so from a distance it looked like the car had collapsed off the jack and trapped someone.

Tubby had come round the corner and the first thing he saw were these legs and immediately thought that Bob was stuck under the car. He rushed forward, panicked and shouting, 'You all right Bob? You all right Bob?' It was only when you were right up close that you could see they were false. Bob said that when Tubby found him he was rather pale, then turned red with anger. It was the first time we had ever known him to be riled. He was livid, calling Bob 'a silly bugger', but as the shock subsided Bob was most relieved that he hadn't given him a heart attack, and they laughed about it over a cup of tea.

He wasn't the only one to fall for it. I once came round the corner and saw those legs. My heart started pounding, rushing into my throat. I rushed forward to see if there was any sign of life and if I could help, my brain racing. I was annoyed to find that I had fallen for another of his pranks.

When I saw Bob he found it highly amusing and just grinned cheekily, saying, 'Got you too!'

Sam separating a pony at Yardworthy, Dartmoor, in 1981

MORE MEMORIES OF SAM

In the weeks and months following the publication of my first book other stories about my father began to come out of the woodwork, from all sorts of different people and places. I've found out more about his early life, too. So before telling the story of my life since leaving the scrapyard at Lettaford, here are a few more tales about my father, Sam Harris.

NAUGHTY BOY

My father was born in 1915 and was named Leonard James Harris. He never knew his father. He always said he was killed in the First World War and that his mother married at Ashdown and started a new family. When Sam was about eight his grandfather, who was called Sam, died. Granny was lonely so Sam's mother sent him to live with her. The neighbours all thought how much he looked like his grandfather and they all started to call him Sam, and the name stuck.

Granny Harris would walk him to school. Sam never liked school. It was a small village school in Hittisleigh and had only one classroom. You started in the class as a little one and you finished in the same class as a big one. Sam would go in, hang up his hat and bag and go straight out the back door. He would run along on the inside of the hedge as Granny tootled along home.

One day the bigger children noticed what he was doing and chased after him. Sam ran straight into a cornfield at the back of the school. He kept running until he couldn't see over the corn. He couldn't see where he was and spent the whole day walking round the cornfield looking for the hedge, so he could find his way out.

He had a teacher called Miss Kelly. Sam used to sit in a tree and sing a riddle to her, 'Miss Kelly, with the rhubarb belly, sitting on the grass with a trumpet up her arse.' This used to infuriate her; Miss Kelly was a very short lady and she had to have her chair on top of a little box so she could reach her desk.

One day Sam and his classmates moved her chair so one leg was out over the edge of the box; so when Miss Kelly got up on her chair and started wriggling about she crashed to the floor. She was so angry; she knew it was down to Sam. She called him to the front and told him she was going to cane him. She produced a cane from the cupboard and told him to hold out his hand. She took a swipe and Sam grabbed the cane and broke it across his knee. So she fetched another one and he did the same. Miss Kelly was furious. She fetched another one and told she was going to cane him and he was not to break this one as she would pay him to keep his hand out for her to cane. She took a swipe and he grabbed it and broke it. She didn't have any more. She then told him she wouldn't forget, and he was dismissed.

Time went by and one day Sam was racing around the playground with his mates when he tripped and fell into the railings. His head went between the bars and he was well and truly stuck. Miss Kelly hadn't forgotten, and she said, 'Got you now Leonard,' and she drashed his ass for him. Sam couldn't sit down for days.

Sam Harris driving a horse and cart in the late 1930s *Photograph courtesy of Dennis Bater*

30

DENNIS'S STORY

I was helping my friend Roy (see later) to take his two tractors, an Allis-Chalmers B and a 434 International, to a vintage tractor rally in the summer of 2012 at Holsworthy. Here I met Dennis Harvey, who was a friend of Roy's as they both go to ploughing matches.

Dennis told me he knew my father and that he could give me some stories. I eventually got his number and made arrangements to visit him so he could tell me more.

Dennis grew up at Lettaford and used to go and visit his grandparents at Coombe, a mile or so away. They were farmers, and during the war his grandfather rented Sam a few fields. Dennis first met Sam was when he was about six years old. On this particular day Sam was ploughing a field with a horse and plough. Dennis was interested in farming and asked Sam if he could have a go at ploughing. Sam replied, 'Yes boy, have a go.' Dennis remembers how there were no wooden handles on the plough. They had long gone, broken off or rotted away. All that was left were metal handles that tapered down to a point.

Dennis had followed the plough until it caught a stone, flicking the plough handles in the air. One of the sharp points stuck in up under his chin. Dennis ran in crying to his grandparents. He remembers his grandfather saying, 'That's nothing boy,' and rubbing his hands under his chin and spreading the blood.

A few years later Sam moved to Lettaford to start his scrap business down the road from Dennis's home. He remembers when Sam first moved in. He had rented a field from Chris Hill, Dennis's farming neighbour, that was wet, full of brambles and thorn bushes, and not fit for farming.

From his late teens Dennis would work for Sam from time to time as he could drive and had his own lorry (at this time Sam didn't have a lorry and couldn't drive). Sam never called him Dennis but always called him Bob, he never quite knew why. They would load his lorry for scrap. To get a good load on they would put bedsteads along the side boards so they could make a higher load. They would then dray the loads to Moretonhampstead station where they filled railway trucks.

Dennis remembers one load that must have had a bit sticking out. They were going down a steep hill and met an oncoming bus. With a heavy load and not the best of brakes they were not able to stop very well. The bit sticking out caught the bus and ripped it right back through. Sam said, 'Don't stop, keep going!'

Another day Sam said, 'Bob, I got some tank tracks to cut up.' Sam had been to Moretonhampstead and had bought a gross of hacksaw blades (144 blades). The tank was at Postbridge, out on the moor. The army had used it for training and target practice. Sam was going to have it for scrap. Sam told Dennis to cut a piece of track while he went down the other side to cut his, hoping to make it more manageable to carry. They were going through axle blades but not making a mark on the tracks. They spent hours sawing and used up all the blades, but never cut though one piece of track.

This tank had two aluminium Jaguar engines inside. Dennis remembers Sam down inside with a sledgehammer smashing the engines to bits so he got something out of it.

There was a similar job out at Hexworthy, behind the Forest Inn. Sam wanted Dennis to go out with his crawler over the moor to pull a gun turret out from behind the pub. Dennis said he tracked all the way and pulled the turret out. By this time Sam had got gas, but the gun turret was armour-plated and the gas wouldn't cut it. He never knew if Sam got the turret or tank back.

Then there was another time Sam wanted Dennis to tow a car back from Dunsford. Dennis said when they arrived to pick up the car, an Austin 16. It had been in a shed, which had been used for a chicken house and it had been there for a long time. It was covered in chicken shit and feathers and was stinking. They managed to wipe the windscreen off as best as they could, leaving it a little smeary.

Sam was towing it with a rope behind the lorry. They came to the crossroads in the middle of Moretonhampstead and when Sam went to pull away he was crashing the gears and the engine was roaring loudly. With a big lurch he broke the rope and sailed off home. He only realised he didn't have Dennis behind when he got out and called, 'Bob, where are you?' Dennis, being young, was so embarrassed at the state of the car that he got out and stood in a shop doorway pretending it was nothing to do with him, leaving the car stood at the junction. He stayed there until Sam came back for him.

The last time Dennis worked for Sam they had gone out to a contractor's at Liverton. Everything had been sold, and the auctioneers had called Sam to come and buy the remaining scrap. While Sam and the auctioneer were making a deal, Dennis had a look round. There was a heap of old hay and in it something red caught his eye. So he had a closer look and moved the hay, and could see it was the bonnet of a tractor. When the auctioneer had gone he showed Sam. They uncovered it and it was an International 1020 petrol. Sam said it was his as he had bought all the scrap and he was going to have the tractor. Dennis played around with the magneto and got a spark. His lorry was petrol so he syphoned some out and put it into the tractor and swung the starting handle. The tractor started up.

They loaded up the rest of the scrap and took it back to the scrapyard and went back to pick up the tractor. Dennis said he fancied this tractor so said to Sam he would like to buy it. Sam said, 'Make us an offer.' (Don't forget the tractor didn't cost Sam anything). Dennis offered him £20 (a lot of money in the late fifties). Sam agreed, and they shook hands on it. So they took the tractor back to Sam's and unloaded. Dennis was going home for the money and told Sam that he would be back. When Dennis got home, his father wanted him to do a job. It was two or three hours before Dennis could get back to the scrapyard with his money to pay for the tractor.

Dennis arrived at Sam's and saw a big hole in the back axle of the tractor. In asking Sam what happened, Sam told him, 'There's usually a bronze crown wheel, worth a lot of money, in the back but there's not one in there, it's iron'.

Sam had ruined a good tractor and broken a verbal deal, but told Dennis he could still have the tractor. It wasn't any good with a big hole in the back axle. Dennis was rightly upset and told Sam, 'Don't ask me to do anything for you again.' He never worked for Sam from then on.

On showing me his tractor collection Dennis told me if he had bought that tractor he would still have it to this day.

JOCK AND THE SHOTGUN

John Sheridan from Chagford told me a story of how he had bought a shotgun off a man called Jock back in the sixties. Jock was a Scot who had worked for Sam for many years, but he was more times drunk than sober.

This particular day John told me how Jock was drunk as hell and waving his shotgun around, shouting that he saw a rat and he was going to shoot it.

As he took aim, Sam seized the gun off him. The rat that Sam could see was someone walking past an old scrapped car with a dark woolly hat on!

CHRIS JONES

Chris Jones remembers Sam from when he was a young boy. Sam and Chris's father were cousins. Chris said it was in the seventies that his father had made arrangements with Sam to pick him up on a Sunday morning to go to Granny's for dinner.

On this particular Sunday morning they arrived to find Sam as black as your hat. Sam had forgotten they were coming. He said he would be ten minutes. Chris said when he reappeared he was washed and shaven, wearing a new shirt, bib and brace overalls and looking very clean. They set off to Granny's.

After they had dinner they sat in the front room and talked all afternoon. Sam was sat in an armchair, and Granny had a white antimacassar laid over the back of the chair. When it came for them to go Sam got up and left a black shadow where his head had been resting. Chris said it looked like the Turin Shroud.

JOHN WESTLAKE

John Westlake, known as Oxo, remembers a visit to Sam's. He said there was an Austin 7 Sport there which John and his mate decided to take for a spin up the lane. The lane is just a dirt track and, going too fast, they mounted the bank and tipped the car over. They hadn't hurt themselves, just a few scratches and grazes. They pushed the car back onto its four wheels and noticed that one wheel was bust. They went back to Sam and had to tell him that they had tipped the car over and busted a wheel. Sam was more concerned that they weren't hurt – and as for the wheel there would undoubtedly be another one in the yard.

John recalls another episode when he was about fourteen. He and some mates from Moretonhampstead, who were older, were out at the Ring of Bells at North Bovey drinking. Sam was there and was going to give them all a lift home. When it was time to go they were all merry. Sam was driving a Standard Flying 14 car at the time and just as they going up the hill out of North Bovey the car ran out of petrol. The brakes wouldn't hold either and the car rolled back into Mr Leaman's car, leaving a big dent in the door. Fortunately John knew someone in the village who had some spare petrol. After topping up the car they eventually made their way back to Moreton.

John used to work in a local garage and Mr Leaman turned up the next day saying someone had banged into his car last night. John said he kept quiet and didn't let on it was Sam.

Sam Harris in the Tom Cobley Inn, Spreyton, in 1988 *Photograph James Tilly*

MR ENDECOTT

A Mr Endecott from Exeter told me when he was a boy he used to come up to Sam's with his father most Sunday afternoons for parts, and to have a good look round because you never knew what you might find.

He said he came up one Sunday with his father in a 1948 Standard. They spent a few hours looking and when they were heading home up the rough stone lane his father was going a bit too fast and he knocked the exhaust off. They turned round and went back to Sam and took another one off an old car. Sam had everything you wanted!

RICHARD MORRIS

Richard and John Morris started to visit Sam when they were 12 and 13 years old in the late fifties and early sixties. Their father would park at the brook in Jurston and go to sleep in the car while the two of them walked up the lane to the yard. They would have a good time rummaging around.

When they were older Sam would pay them to cut up cars. They would get £1 a car. Richard tells of a time that someone went to pinch a car radiator. Sam had been talking to Richard and said, 'I won't be long', and disappeared. It wasn't long until Sam was back with a radiator in his hand. He carried on talking like nothing had happened and didn't say anything about the radiator. When Richard spoke to Dave, Sam's workman, later that evening Dave told him how Sam had walked straight up to the person pinching the radiator, punched him, picked up the radiator and walked off! Even to this day Richard feels it was fair, as matey was going to steal the radiator.

He remembers a time when his brother John would often buy a car a month from Sam. John could buy a car for 'fiver and chop', which meant you could trade in your own car. It might smoke a bit, or it might have had a rattle, a short MOT or only a bit of road tax left, but he would drive it on until he found another one which was better.

It was wet one morning so the two of them went to Sam's. Sam's place, being closer to the moor, was even wetter. He had just received a load of cast aluminium gearboxes from buses. Sam told them he would pay £2.50 per hundredweight if the boys could clean the gearboxes. They made arrangements to take them home and break them in the dry. They started by undoing the nuts and bolts with spanners but found this took them too long to earn any money, so they decided to break them with a sledgehammer. They separated the clean aluminium from the iron and were back up at Sam's by late morning and had earned £12.50, which was good money back then.

Richard tells of a time he bought a Vauxhall Victor which had rusted around the headlights. He fixed the headlights up by packing newspaper around the lights and filling it with fibreglass. He kept the car for six or seven years before selling it back to Sam. He said the body of the car was completely rusted out but the headlights were still solid. Sam gave him £7 for the car. When he got home his neighbour asked him what he had done with his car. Richard replied, 'Sold it to Sam and he's given me £7 for it for scrap'. His neighbour said, 'I would have given you £7 just for the tyres.' Richard said, 'I'll go back up Sam's and get them then.'

Richard remembers another time when a local sergeant and constable arrived in their police car outside Sam's gate. He couldn't believe his eyes. Sam had gone straight up to the police car and peed on the back left wheel while they were still sat in it. (There was a law that you could pee on the left-hand rear wheel of any vehicle as long as you placed your left hand on the car while you did so.) Richard felt Sam didn't like these officers much and it was as if he was marking his territory.

Richard and Sam went out picking up scrap and they came across a couple of men from the National Park fixing up a stone stile. Sam turned to Richard and said that he and the farmer had only just recently put the stile back together. Richard took it that Sam must have knocked it down.

Derek White with his Dad on Dartmoor *Photograph courtesy of Derek White*

DEREK WHITE'S MEMORIES

My Dad found Sam's when he got his first car in 1955, when I was six. It was a 1930s Austin 7. I can still remember the registration, OU6 676. My Mum would pack a Sunday picnic and we would head for Sam's from Tavistock. We would stop at the river at the head of the lane, where Mum would stay with the car, and Dad and I would walk, armed with a tool bag, to collect bits for the cars running restoration.

When we were about to leave, Sam would come out of his caravan with a black mug of tea in his hand. Dad would usually stay talking for what seemed like hours to me, then Dad would pay up. Sam would look at me and ask, 'What have you got then?' Being always told to be honest I said, 'A clock.' He would take it off me and wind it and if it did not work (which they never did) he would give it to me with a big smile.

These trips were so regular; we must have made one a month until the early 1960s when MOT tests came in. Dad then had an

Austin A40 Somerset. I can remember the yard and lane stacked full of cars, all MOT failures. During one of these visits we met Jock. Dad had driven up the lane as we needed something that was heavy to carry. Jock spied us coming and came to greet us. 'That's a fine car,' he said, 'what's the engine like?' So Dad let him sit inside; he started it up and placed his foot on the floor. After what seemed like an hour of the engine screaming its head off, he switched off and said, 'That's a good engine.' I always had a laugh with my Dad years later over this as, being an engineer, I now know if the engine had gone BANG it would have been a bad one!

We had quite a few scrapyards around Tavistock, but we always went to Sam's because, according to my Dad, the prices were always reasonable. This I found out when I needed a gearbox for my first car, a Morris 1000 van. Local yards wanted over £10 which, and as an apprentice on £6 a week, I could not afford. So a trip to Sam's got one for £2 (it did have the traditional Morris 1000 first gear, though, which I lived with).

After our long walk back down the lane, we would get handfuls of fine sand from the river to rub the black oil off our hands (Swarfega had not been invented back then). Then we would do the same with our oily wellies. After this we would sit down to eat our sandwiches (with the odd thumbprint if the oil was really black!).

In September 1995 my Dad died suddenly, and Mum asked me to clear the garage. In a box I found some of the clocks Sam had given me, but as these were beyond my skills, they still didn't work!

Peggy's daughter Clare with her snowman at Great Ley, Upton Pyne *Photograph courtesy of Peggy Harris*

THE YEARS THAT STANK

Before leaving the scrapyard I met a person – actually I'd known him for years. He was a lot older than me and I used to see him and his family at the weekend. He told me the relationship was over between him and his ex-woman, but that they stayed together for the children.

I was young and very green. He wormed his way around me. I was the 'best thing since sliced bread' in his life, so he said. He was the first person to show me kindness; he was warm, gentle and happy-go-lucky. Nothing was ever too much trouble; he often gave me a hand and helped me out. I knew he had been violent to one of his ex-women, but he blamed her; she had 'driven' him to it.

I won't use my ex-partner's name; let's just call him 'Stinker'.

OUT OF THE FRYING PAN AND INTO THE FIRE

I had been going with him for several months before I started to see the true person. I was beginning to have second thoughts but found I was pregnant – too late. I felt I couldn't tell my mother as we had never talked about anything. I was still too scared of her. I couldn't face dealing with the problem and carried on as normal, hoping it would go away. I thought she might have made me get rid of it and I couldn't face dealing with that. So I kept my pregnancy to myself and worked full-time in the scrapyard loading and unloading lorries, picking up scrap and throwing it around.

I was too scared to go to the doctor until I was seven months gone. Until then I acted like I wasn't pregnant but I was careful. I tried to do most of the lifting with my arm muscles so as not to damage my baby.

I remember one particular day when I was sent to Moretonhampstead to pick up a cast-iron bath. The owner and I carried it down three flights of stairs; I went backwards, lifting the bath down step by step. The man was holding it back and I just hoped he wouldn't let go as I was more than six months gone. We got it down and between us lifted it onto the back of the pickup.

I hadn't been to the doctor many times in my life but at seven months I thought I ought to; I was terrified. On entering the room he asked how he could help me. I told him I was pregnant. His reply was, 'How do you know that?' as I wasn't showing. I was all round but didn't show until the last month. He told me to lie on the bed so he could examine my tummy. He asked me if I was going to marry the father. I told him I wasn't. The doctor didn't seem to like my answer and was rougher with the rest of his examination. He pushed his hand hard on the base of my stomach, causing me pain for the next two days. I hadn't had any pain like it before. I had a hospital appointment for my first scan a few days later. I moved to a different surgery as I wasn't going back for any more of his rude behaviour and rough treatment.

I was in this on my own, and didn't feel I could go talk to anyone in my family. I was pregnant out of wedlock. I thought I would be condemned as they were very Victorian in their views.

Mother left the yard for good when I was about seven months pregnant. She asked me to take her to Exeter. As we drove along I wanted to tell her; it was on the tip of my tongue for the entire journey. I wanted to say, 'Mum, I'm pregnant, don't leave' – but I couldn't. I just drove her to Sowton services with a big lump in my throat. I was still scared and we were never affectionate with each other. Since then I've thought she knew and was just leaving me to it.

Stinker told me he was going to tell Sam I was pregnant, now that Mother had gone. He arranged to meet with Father; he was going to take him out for the day. Somewhere out over the moor he pulled up and said he had something to tell Sam, and if he didn't like it he could lump it or walk home. 'Peggy's pregnant and I'm the father.' Father's reply was, 'How did you manage that?' (I was known for being rather stand-offish and a bit of a hot head.) 'I'd better lump it then as I don't want to walk home.'

The next day Father said to me, 'Well, you're not the first and won't be the last – if it's a boy call it Sam.' I was so pleased that Father was being kind about it, but it didn't last. By the next month he was calling me a slut and a tart and other nasty names which cut deep, so I left. I was away for a week until Father sent Bob to ask me to come back. Father said he was sorry, so I went back. He was very apologetic and was crying. I had never seen him like this before. I thought he meant it, but a few weeks later he was calling me names again.

Towards the end of the pregnancy Stinker had a Ford Transit van which he was scrapping, but he wanted to keep the engine. He told me to take the engine out and take it to his house. You never questioned him, or refused; you just did as you were told.

I took the front off the van and undid all the bolts around the gearbox (I was about eight months at this time). I had to go under the van to undo the last of the housing bolts. While I was lying on my back under the van the baby started to move, and when I tried to slide back out I found I was stuck. I had to shout for someone to pull me out – it was his ex. I lifted the V4 Transit engine out onto the floor. His ex (I'll call her Number Two) said she was going to help me to get it onto the pickup. It was heavy; I could only lift it knee-high but managed to get it waist-high with her help. A stranger passing by saw us struggling so he gave us a hand. He turned to me and said, 'You shouldn't be lifting engines in your condition,' but he didn't know that if I hadn't got it there I would be in bigger trouble. I delivered the engine to where I'd been told, but then Stinker just bollocked me for doing it in my condition – I couldn't win.

I talked to Number Two as I was going to have to live with her because Stinker said I wasn't to bring the baby up in the scrapyard. He threatened that he would have the baby taken away if I went home. She told me bits and pieces about what to expect about giving birth but it wasn't anywhere near what I experienced.

I was due on 25 September. I had been to hospital that day and had been given a kick chart to monitor the baby. Stinker was going off for an MOT that evening and told me to stay and look after his kids as I was too close to my time. The kids were suffering with sickness and diarrhoea. I was sat at the table having tea. He was restless and started messing about. He pulled me up by my chin, and backwards over the chair. I felt my spine snick, causing a sharp pain in the middle of my back. Trying to hide the pain from him, I slowly moved to a soft chair in the front room. He left with Number Two, leaving me for three hours to look after the kids. Gradually the pain started to move round to the front of my belly and I started to feel unwell. The pain would come and go. I didn't realise I was going into labour; I just thought I was coming down with what the kids had.

Stinker came back in a better mood; the car had passed the MOT, much to my relief. Number Two noticed me twinging and, recognising the signs of labour, rang for an ambulance.

By the time the ambulance arrived my contractions had increased to every two minutes. I went in alone. They drove up to Whiddon Down, which was under construction for a new bypass. They had dug up the old roundabout, leaving the road very bumpy. As we bounced along I thought I was going to give birth there and then. The ambulance men tried to put me at ease and said, 'It's been a long time since we have had a baby born in here.' 'I ain't having a baby in here!' I replied.

Arriving at the hospital, I had no idea what was happening. I was young, frightened and alone with strangers. I was being strapped to machines, an enema shoved up my bum. After five minutes I needed to go to the toilet. The nurse said I had to wait as they were taking a heart trace of the baby. I waited for a while but still needed to go and asked again. 'In a minute dear,' was her reply. 'If you don't let me go, I'll shit the bed!' I don't mince my words, so we sorted that problem. About half an hour later another nurse came, put on a pair of rubber gloves and said she was going to do an internal. I didn't know what she meant until she started. I found myself saying, 'You dirty bugger, what do you think your doing?!' Then she explained. During the labour a young nurse told me to hold her hand. After a strong contraction I looked over at her. She was in great pain as I had squeezed her hand so tight her hand disappeared inside of mine. I had a very strong grip! The poor thing never held my hand for the rest of the labour.

After Clare was born I had to have stitches after 16¼ hours' labour. I was in and out of consciousness from all the drugs. There was a voice asking if I wanted a cup of tea. I opened my eyes to look to see where the voice had come from, and there between my knees I could see someone sewing. I replied in a weary voice, 'Not with you there.'

I stayed in the hospital for five days. The day after Clare was born my Aunty Angel and Cousin Ann came to see me. They had heard a rumour round Chagford that Sam Harris's daughter was pregnant. Angel had rung Father and he had said that I'd had a baby girl that morning. Like I said, I hadn't told anyone. My heart dropped as I saw my aunt walk through the door as I thought Nan, my grandmother, would be following; she was quite Victorian in her ways. I was so relieved to see Ann instead. After looking at the baby, Angel reassured me everything would be OK but I would have to see Nan the next day, as she was bringing her to see me. She reassured me that Nan was all right about the situation and not to worry – but I still did.

The next day Angel brought Nan. I felt embarrassed and slightly ashamed as I thought she would look down on me for getting pregnant out of wedlock, but she was very kind and understanding with no questions. She greeted me warmly, reassuring me that these things sometimes happened and that I wasn't to worry. She liked babies and cooed over her great-granddaughter. She asked me what she was called. I replied, 'Clare.' She asked if I had given her a middle name, but I hadn't. Angel suggested I called her Marie. So my baby became Clare Marie but Nan called her 'Lady Clare Marie' and told me I was to bring her up like a lady – as I grew up a tomboy. She often referred to her as Lady Clare Marie from then on. Stinker didn't bother to visit; he said he would see the baby when it came home.

The day I came home I was staying out in Hittisleigh. Stinker had picked up Father to come and see the baby. They talked until two in the morning. Stinker was too tired to drive Father home so I had to take him and on the way Father told me I was working in the morning. So I had to go back to work. I was so weak; I had lost all my strength. It took me several weeks to get over it all – I was just so knackered.

Stinker had changed. I had to be back from work at 5.30pm, 6.45 at the latest – there'd be trouble else.

He started to knock me around. I had Clare at the end of September. One day I came home very tired, sore from work. He wasn't working at the time. He was bored and thought he would play rough with me. I told him to get off. He stood in front of me saying, 'Come on. Get up and hit me in the belly, come on,' slapping his belly in temptation. I refused. This annoyed him so he started to hurt me by grabbing my head and digging his nails into my chin and jerking my head from side to side. This pissed me off. I jumped up ready to strike; this took him by surprise but then angered him. I saw his face change so I dropped my hands, but it was too late. Now he was going to teach me a lesson. He smacked me around and knocked me to the ground, banging the back of my head on the fireplace. His ten-year-old son told me the next day that Stinker had pulled me out of the fire and had booted me around the floor, kicking me in the stomach and back. All I remember is him standing over me shouting, 'Get up, else I'll pour this water over you.' He had a bowl of water in his hands. In the first week of November I got my Aunt Angel to take me to the osteopath in Exeter as I had put my back and neck out in five places when I had hit the fireplace.

I lived in fear of being late, of saying or doing the wrong thing. He smacked me around numerous times for silly reasons. He left me with a black eye once. Brother Bob noticed the black eye and passed comment. I passed it off that I had been playing with the kids and got head butted. I found myself covering for him.

I was embarrassed. It was like he'd brainwashed me: it was always my fault, I made him hit me, I asked for it. I had nowhere to go. He told me that I wasn't taking Clare. If I left he would tell Social Services I was an unfit mother. He kept me in fear. I wasn't the only one he treated like this: he did it to his ex-women as well. It had all been a lie. He wasn't staying with his ex-women for the kids; he was still with them. I was Number Four. He wasn't going to change, other than to get worse.

People always say, 'I wouldn't put up with someone knocking me around, I would soon kick them out or be up the road myself.' It's not as easy as that; they get in your head, I don't know how. Maybe it was because I was young and vulnerable. He manipulated me by being caring, gentle, a good listener – all the things I was looking for; it was like he was fishing and he just reeled me in. After the baby was born it all changed. I was stuck. He told me in a calm collected tone that if I had an accident or became disfigured he wouldn't want me any more; I was his now and he was the boss.

He would exercise his authority on us regularly. At times he would command that we kiss his shoes. When he first did it to me I refused and he twisted my arm up my back and put pressure on my hands, bending them into my wrists. With his other hand around the back of my neck he pushed me to the floor until my face touched his shoes, saying sternly, 'Kiss my shoes.' I just pretended to. It was as if he just enjoyed the power trip, and it was easier to give in.

He liked to slap you when you told him something he didn't want to hear, even if it was the truth. His hands were like lightning. Your nose and mouth would be bleeding and you would just feel the pain. He would always plead poor and suggested I was to buy him steak and biscuits as I had child benefit and he wanted it. I paid my share of the housekeeping and rent. When I wasn't working I was to drive him wherever he needed to go. Slowly he was taking more and more out of me. Then he had the cheek to blame me he was getting fat.

The abuse gradually got worse. He humiliated us, blamed, brainwashed or would just beat us. It was always our fault; we made him do it, we asked for it, we made him like that.

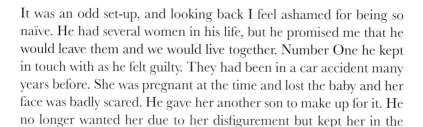

It was an odd set-up, and looking back I feel ashamed for being so naïve. He had several women in his life, but he promised me that he would leave them and we would live together. Number One he kept in touch with as he felt guilty. They had been in a car accident many years before. She was pregnant at the time and lost the baby and her face was badly scared. He gave her another son to make up for it. He no longer wanted her due to her disfigurement but kept her in the circle for her son's sake.

Number Two had four children but only three were his. He told me he had beaten her as she had stolen from him and she had driven him to it. He had beaten her with electric cable. He only kept in contact with her because of the children. Number Three didn't have any children from him at the time. He wanted to leave her as she too had stolen off him, but he was just staying with her to get his money back. In my naïvety at the beginning I thought he would never need to hit me as I would never give him cause to.

It was too late when I realised that it was all lies and that he wasn't going to give any of them up. Number Three gave birth to a boy one month after I had Clare. He made me live with Number Two as he thought she could help me with the baby. I had nowhere else to go. It was a three-bedroom house, and I had the box room with Clare. Number Two had her own room and the kids shared the second, while he lived in another village a few miles away.

Number Two's eldest girl wasn't his. She was very nervy and would often wet the bed twice a night. She would put on a brave face and seem to be happy-go-lucky but underneath I knew she was petrified of him. I would wake her up in the night to get her to go to the toilet, but she would still wet the bed.

He had a soft spot for the middle girl as she would try to please him and be a tomboy. He would make her fight with the other children to toughen them up; fight until they were crying or blood was drawn. This was like sport to him. She was a good kid and was often sent with me to be a chaperone and report back.

These two girls would hang around me and help me with Clare. One of them would always come and take Clare in the morning and dress her so I could sleep on until I had to go to work.

They were like two little mums who were always helping out and looking after the little ones. I would reward them with sweets and biscuits. On one occasion, when Clare was really poorly, she had vomited everywhere. I was cleaning the cot when the eldest one walked in and offered to help clean up. As it was a terrible job I said I would pay her 50p (quite a lot of money back then). She did it without any complaints as she was so desperate for the money. I felt so bad about it I gave her £1 and some sweets instead.

The youngest daughter was a frail, quiet, shy little girl with a runny nose who would climb up on my lap. She was known as Daddy's little girl; she was born premature as he'd beaten the mother during her pregnancy. She was born with bad hips and spent a lot of time in plaster when she was very young. Stinker felt guilty that she was born that way. She would always come by my room looking for sweets.

The boy was spoilt and had terrible temper tantrums. He was treated like the man of the house; he couldn't do anything wrong. He was a nice little boy until Stinker would show up. He would bring the worst out of him and encourage him.

On the whole they were all nice little kids, although you could tell they would all grow up with issues.

I have seen the middle girl a few times since I left and she is still getting treatment for her traumatic childhood. She always says I should have taken her with me. I wish I could have but it was not possible. She said that after I left he turned more on the children. Within two years of me leaving most of the kids had been taken into care, and Number One and Two also left him.

I understand he still lives with Number Three who has given him three children. I've heard down the grapevine over the years that he still beats her occasionally.

When I left it took me several years but I now realise what a weak, pathetic man he actually is. He is a waste of space, a drain on society and I pity those who are not strong enough to realise this.

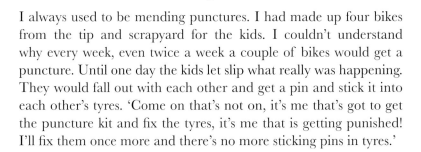

I always used to be mending punctures. I had made up four bikes from the tip and scrapyard for the kids. I couldn't understand why every week, even twice a week a couple of bikes would get a puncture. Until one day the kids let slip what really was happening. They would fall out with each other and get a pin and stick it into each other's tyres. 'Come on that's not on, it's me that's got to get the puncture kit and fix the tyres, it's me that is getting punished! I'll fix them once more and there's no more sticking pins in tyres.'

MOTHERHOOD

After having Clare I sat in the hospital ward watching all the new mothers kissing and cooing over their newborn babies. On my first day a nurse showed me how to feed, wind and change Clare, then later on how to bath her. I was shell-shocked as I had never handled a baby in my life and didn't have a clue. I was 19 but young for my age. I felt numb.

I had started to see a side of Stinker I didn't like. Part of me was realising I was in a situation I had no control over. The labour was traumatising as I had no idea what to expect. I was relieved I had given birth to a pretty, healthy baby as I knew he wouldn't have been happy with me if I hadn't, and then he wouldn't want us.

It is hard for me to express my emotions. Growing up I was never shown love or affection, and I had never felt loving emotions. Things were either OK or bad. I sat in the hospital bed watching Clare breathing in her cot. She was dainty – a pretty baby with long slender fingers, like a china doll. I'd always felt ugly and was proud she was so pretty. Nan had said I had to bring her up as a lady. I sat thinking about life and decided I would do the best I could for her and make sure she didn't end up like me, always struggling.

I may have found it hard to show my emotions but I knew I could never let her go. It couldn't have been obvious on the outside as the nurses asked if I wanted her. But I wasn't going to give her up.

I had Number Two visiting and reporting back. The nurses were a little concerned and spoke to Number Two who had told them I was going home with her. She'd said before I had given birth that she would help me with the baby as she had four kids herself. The nurse who did the home visit was concerned I wasn't showing very much emotion. I wasn't very verbal. Number Two told her I was just shy and that she would hear me talking in the night, when I thought everyone was asleep.

I couldn't ask questions but my gut reaction was that things were not right at home. Clare was the bottom of the pecking order. Number Two was ordered to look after Clare but I felt she wasn't 100 percent nice to her. In front of anyone she was the doting mother; she could turn on the charm, the kissing, the cooing and cuddling. Behind closed doors, when I left, the other children told me she would often shout at my baby and keep her in bed all day.

When I got back from work I would sit in the front room with my dinner on my lap and Clare would always come to my knee and pick off my plate. I never stopped her as I felt she must have been hungry. Number Two would always say, 'She's had her tea, I've fed her.'

Some time later on, when we had been in the refuge (see below) for a few months, I mentioned Number Two's name to Clare. She became hysterical and ran off, terrified, as if the woman was about to enter the room. It confirmed my suspicions.

I would always have her in the evenings and during the nights unless I had to take Stinker out. Clare was an easy baby; it was as if she knew and made life easier for me. When she was really small I would lay her on my chest and doze off with her as I was so exhausted. I cherished our private time, but it was as if Stinker didn't want me to spend much time with her as he would insist I was to drive him and take him places.

I found it hard being a new mother, especially when I had to go straight back to work. I had to let another woman look after my baby. I was put out because Clare was encouraged to call another woman 'Mummy'.

From when Clare could speak she always called me Peggy but mostly 'My Peggy.' She never called me Mummy; she always called Number Two 'Mummy'. I remember saying to Stinker one evening that Clare only called me by my name and called Number Two Mummy. I was annoyed about it but it was difficult. I couldn't really say much about it. Stinker's reply was, 'Number Two is more of a mother than you are.' He wasn't going to change things.

When I met Margaret in the refuge she asked me why Clare called me by my name. I told her that was what Clare's father wanted, about Number Two and how I had to work every day to support us. She felt it was wrong that a toddler was calling her mother by her Christian name so from then on she always spoke to Clare referring to me as her Mummy, telling her that I was her Mummy and that she was to call me Mummy. Slowly and surely she did.

In her mid-teens she decided to call me Peggy again, which hit a nerve. With a short reply I growled, 'I am your Mum.' She always called me Mum after that, but Mummy when she was creeping.

It was a really cold winter in 1986. It was so cold at night I would have Clare's bottle made up and wrap it in a towel and keep it in bed with me so it kept warm. There was no heating in the house apart from an open fire in the front room. I would wrap Clare in layers of clothes and cover her in plenty of bedding. I would warm the bed with a hot-water bottle before laying her down. When she woke in the night her little face was frozen. After feeding and changing her she would get cold so I would tuck her in with me. I know it wasn't wise but it was so cold. She would purr with contentment as she suckled my heat.

One night all the pipes froze in the bathroom. We woke up to water running down the stairs. I found the stopcock and turned it off. This meant there was no water in the house. I hunted the garden for the hosepipe and it was frozen stiff. I cut lengths off it and cut the leaky parts of the burst water pipes out and replaced them with the hose and jubilee clips so that we had water as there were two adults, four kids and a baby in the house. It was few days before the plumber came and a while before the house dried out.

BURNT BABY

One hot summer's day in 1987, Stinker was planning to be outside all day, digging and gardening. He told me that he was going to have Clare sat in a pushchair out with him. She was around ten months old, and had been fed and changed. The sun was rising and I sat her in the shade. It was already warm, and it was only half light in the morning. I remember saying, 'Don't forget to move her when the sun moves.' His reply was, 'She's all right, I won't forget,' so I left for work.

That evening when I got back home I couldn't believe my eyes. Half of Clare's face was bright red; she was burnt all down one side.

He had left her in the sun. I wanted to shout, 'What the f*****g hell was you thinking of, letting her get burnt?' but I had to bite my tongue and ask politely what had happened to her. He just said, 'She was so quiet I forgot her.'

TURNED OVER A CAR

I had gone over to Bow early one morning to fill up with petrol and I had to leave Clare with her father. It has been hot weather for weeks. I went the back way out of Bow up through Spreyton. The road is windy and narrow. All of a sudden the gear brake bust, and all I had was third gear. I knew that around the corner there was a fairly steep hill under trees. I accelerated up but met a big four-wheeled tractor. As it had been so dry the trees had dropped sap and the road had become slippery. So when I started to brake – as I was unable to change down a gear – I started to go into a slide. All I could see was a small gap and a very large tractor. I thought I would aim for the hedge as I might get hurt hitting the tractor.

It all happened in slow motion. I could see the left front wheel arch folding inwards from the impact, coming across the floor at me. Then lifting, onto my side… it felt like flying. I was waiting for the bang from crashing into the tractor. My car hit the ground on one side and tipped onto its roof, throwing me around. I landed on the car windscreen on my hands and knees on the road. The petrol was running down the car. I had to crawl out from under the bonnet, but the gap was too small.

Luckily two men turned up in a pickup and pulled open the door and helped me get to my feet. I glanced at the pickup and saw they had a headstone in the back. They were gravediggers! I thanked them and smiled, saying, 'I don't need you yet.' They laughed.

Stinker was more upset as I had promised to give him the car at the weekend and now it was scrap.

EMPTY SAFE

Stinker told me how he had stolen a safe and a minivan from a butcher's shop. He had put the safe into the back of the minivan and taken it onto the moor where he bashed it open with an axe. To his disappointment there wasn't anything in it. He was so angry he smashed the van to pieces and chopped it up into bits.

To add an extra sting in the tail a few days later the local newspaper stated that the safe had contained several hundred pounds. Stinker knew the butcher. He would jest to him that the safe was empty. The butcher was laughing, 'Only them who robbed it would know!'

STINKER'S VAN

Stinker had a red Transit van and decided to sell it to Father as the engine had gone. He had bought an engine off his brother for £40 but couldn't be bothered to put it in. I bought the van off Father and bought the engine from Stinker, took out the old engine and put in the new one. I spent all day struggling; they're not easy to lift on your own.

I turned the keys and after a while of whizzing it fired up, but to my disappointment after all my hard work it wasn't any good. It rattled like a bag of nails. I was upset I had wasted money on an old van and a knackered engine. When I told Stinker that the engine was no good he started to rant that he had been ripped off. He was going to tell his brother that he wanted his money back. Well, his brother never paid up and it was me who had really lost out.

STINKER'S FATHER
AND THE SECONDHAND TYRES

Stinker's father was a brute of a man. He often said his father would beat him and his brothers with a belt when they were little. He told me how his father would just point his thumb up to the ceiling to signal it was time for them to go to bed. If they made any noise he would be up with a belt.

When I knew his father he was just an old man with bad health. He was very keen on visiting the bookies each week. Stinker asked me if I could get a couple of old tyres with decent tread to give to his father so he could sell them on to make a few quid (I could have done with the money and him not wasting it like that). He wasn't really asking; he was telling me that was what he wanted me to do. If I didn't produce any, that would be wrong. So I gave in and got him three, knowing that this wouldn't be the last of it because the old man would be expecting more the next time he saw me.

A couple of weeks passed before I had to take Stinker down to see his parents. It wasn't long before the subject of tyres came up. Stinker's father said, 'You know those tyres you gave me? They weren't any good.' 'What do you mean?' I replied, 'they were good tyres.' The old man said, 'You come and see for yourself.' The tone of his voice had changed because I had questioned him.

So we went out to his van and he showed me three very worn and perished tyres. 'These aren't the tyres I gave you, these are worn out!' 'I told you, they aren't any good, you have to replace them as you have made look like a bloody fool when I was selling them to my buyer.'

I told him, 'They aren't my tyres. These are covered in red mud and the tyres I gave you were covered in black dirt. The soil in our area is black, not red!'

He was furious; he went in and snapped and snarled at Stinker, and was in a foul mood for the rest of the evening. Stinker tried to sweeten him up by giving him a £20 note. He growled, 'She is calling me a bloody liar!' I wasn't; I just pointed out they weren't mine and I wasn't replacing tyres which weren't mine.

We had to leave early. Stinker was in a shitty mood on the way home and told me off for upsetting his father. He told me I was to give him more tyres, but I left soon after.

WHAT STINKER TOLD ME

One dark winter evening when visiting his parents on the other side of Tavistock Stinker took me to a wood with some buildings in it. He told me it was a drying mill. He bragged about how he had wrecked the machinery in it, and why.

He told me how his father and brother had called in one day and asked the owner if he had any scrap. The owner was not polite and told them to clear off as he didn't want gypsies calling in. They obviously spoke to each other and decided to go back one night and teach this chap a lesson.

They wrecked and stole anything they could get off the site, and damaged what they couldn't. The owner of the mill would have had a big expense. He managed to get it all up and running again, but Stinker wasn't satisfied with the damage he had done. He went back months later and did more. He put dirt in the fuel tanks and smashed everything again. The owner couldn't afford to get it going again, and all because he had called them gypsies. I know it's true because when I met Roy (see below) he told me how he used to work in a corn-drying place and it closed down due to vandals. He said it was hit twice and people had lost their jobs, and that he had bought the lorry from the mill, and how the lorry wouldn't run as there was dirt in the fuel tank.

One evening Stinker's son, who was about nine at the time, told me how Daddy had hit a man from next door and he was lying in the wheelbarrow for a long time. Daddy had pushed him to his back door and left him there.

Another time he told me how Number Three had pissed him off. She had some ducks so he dragged her down the garden and made her watch while he chopped their heads off with an axe. He was telling her it was better them than her.

I CHASED THE JEHOVAH'S WITNESSES

For years I went to the same school as the Jehovah's Witness kids. The eldest boy was the same age as me; he was called Philip Buttle. One autumn morning we were all stood outside the Pepper Pot in the middle of Chagford waiting for the coach to go to Okehampton school. I often had kids poking fun or laughing at me, but this particular morning with no warning Philip Buttle, this God-fearing creature, decided I needed a wash. He had picked up a bucket of dirty smelly water that had been used to wash the toilet floor in the gents. He said I was dirty and took the bucket and threw it over me, and all the silly boys stood and laughed. I didn't think it was funny. I couldn't go to school as I was cold and wet and smelling of disinfectant. I didn't want to go home as it was hard enough for Mother to wash and dry clothes once a week for school as we didn't have a washing machine or tumble dryer. So I decided to catch the minibus back to my Nan's as the minibus owner lived next door. Nan couldn't believe that this boy could have done such a thing; she got my Aunty to clean and dry my uniform.

Time went by. I was now an adult and a new mother. I used to leave my baby daughter Clare with Number Two out at Hittisleigh while I went to work. I found out that two Jehovah's Witnesses used to visit her once a week, on a Wednesday. I came back early one day and they were bouncing my baby on their knees. They told me they were having prayers. I didn't mind if they had faith but I didn't want them praying over my daughter. I told Number Two my views; I told her I would get my mother or aunt to have the baby on Wednesdays (I didn't want Number Two to miss out on the Jehovah's Witnesses' company as she was lonely).

Blow me! I found that they deliberately changed their day to a Thursday so that they could see the baby. This annoyed me.

One evening when I returned to Number Two's I saw a pile of books. I picked up one; they were Jehovah books. She said that the Jehovah's Witnesses had given them to her free of charge.

The next day when I went to work the Jehovah's Witnesses were up at the scrapyard selling the same books to my Father. They wanted £25. I told Father, 'You don't want these books 'cause you won't read them.' These two Jehovah's Witnesses stood there and told Father that he would have a thousand years to live after death. This was the last straw. I turned and told them, 'How can you live after a thousand years after death when you're dead? You're dead!'

Then they started on me, how they were going to pray for me and that Jehovah was looking down on me. I told them both to leave, 'Get out!' They just stood there preaching. I told them I would count to ten and if they hadn't left I would throw a bucket of dirty water over them. With that I picked up a bucket and started counting, 'One, two…' Damn, they were out on ten. This annoyed me, as I wanted to throw a bucket of water over them, as it was the youngest girl's brother who'd done the same to me all those years before.

They had arrived in a red three-wheeler car. They were in no hurry to leave; they ambled back to their car and started to reverse slowly to turn round in the lane.

I was so wound up I jumped into my pickup and drove at them. I wouldn't let them turn round; I made them reverse all the up the rough track to the farm, about a quarter of a mile. I was inches away from their bumper. They both looked frightened as I hurled abuse out of my window, shouting to them never to return.

I don't think they'll preach to a woman suffering from post-natal depression ever again.

Tired and exhausted: the first week at the refuge *Photograph courtesy of Peggy Harris*

Clare dressing up Old Reg, who Peggy and Clare met when they left the refuge and moved into a bedsit in Exete
Photograph courtesy of Peggy Harris

LIVING AT THE REFUGE

Eventually Stinker's treatment of me got so bad I became really scared for what might happen to us if we stayed. I just couldn't take any more. I explain how me and Clare ended up at the woman's refuge in Exeter in 'The day I went back to the yard' in the 'Time at Great Ley' chapter.

I arrived at the refuge on 18 June 1988, just before midday. I was battered, very bruised and scarred for life. I was 21, and Clare was just 18 months old. She was clinging very tight to me, wide-eyed and very scared too.

We both arrived in the clothes we stood up in. I had a small suitcase with only personal things, baby photos, driving licence, birth certificates, Clare's moneybox, but no clothes.

THE PINK HOUSE

It was a Wednesday. It is vague in my memory but I remember being greeted at the door. It was loud, with lots of kids running around and their mothers sitting smoking and talking. The building was well worn and well lived in but I didn't care; it was safe. One lady, a worker, helped me settle in. She showed me my room and informed me of the house rules as she introduced me to the other women, the main rule being, 'No men are allowed in the house'.

It was a lot to take in and I found it overwhelming. They gave me a cup of tea and said there was a meeting that afternoon. My head was splitting; I had such a bad headache. I was sore, bruised and – thinking back on it – suffering from concussion. I would drift in and out of consciousness.

After the meeting I was advised to go to the hospital to make a record of the injuries I had. The nurse wanted me to get the police involved and press charges but I was too scared as Stinker had threatened to have Clare taken off me. I didn't want him to find us. As I settled myself in my room, a lady came and introduced herself. She was little and spoke with an air of superiority. I thought she was another worker. She told me I was to go into town to buy some toiletries.

I had never really been to Exeter, only to Marsh Barton a few times to the scrapyard. The refuge was nearly in the middle of town. I had only ever been into town once, to Thomas Moore's when I was 11 to buy school uniform.

She walked me up to Boots and was very inquisitive about my personal life and it was only a few days later I realised she was no different from myself, another battered woman. I felt cheated as she had conned me into divulging my personal situation.

Clare was very unsettled, shy and timid. She stuck to me like glue, literally. She had to be sitting on my lap all the time, even when I went to the bathroom. I couldn't put her to bed; she would insist on sleeping under my arm in the chair all evening. It took her a long time to come out of her shell and be able to be left on her own again. It was several months before I could prise Clare from my lap and leave her to play with the other small children.

I did leave Clare for three days, as I had to go into hospital to be treated for concussion as I kept passing out. The headaches were unbearable. My aunt was notified that I was in there. She brought my mother up with her. Mother told me I was to imagine sheep were the headache in my head. I was to send a dog in and round them up and send them out between my eyebrows – what a help!

I suffered with crippling headaches for two-and-half-years until I received treatment from a cranial osteopath. I still suffer with them to this day.

The house could change on a daily basis but sometimes it would be weeks before you would see a new face or someone would leave. There was a real mix of characters, from all walks of life; from 17 right up to their eighties, from babies to teenagers.

It was sad. Sometimes women would come in and stay just a few days, or hours even. They couldn't handle leaving their homes and family. Then there were people like me who were never going back and were determined to start a new life.

I believe if I hadn't had the refuge Clare and I would be dead. I believe he would have put us down the mineshaft like he promised.

THE DREAM

I had been in the refuge for a couple of months. I had telephoned home a few times to speak to Father but Stinker would cut into the call and I would put the phone down. It was nearly the end of September when I had this dream – more like a nightmare. I dreamt that Father had been neglected, and was laying on the kitchen floor with froth coming from his nose, which meant pneumonia to me. He spoke to me and his words were, 'I'm dying Peg.' It was so real I woke up shaking, jumped out of bed and looked for some change and rushed downstairs to the phone. I rang home as the dream had shaken me up. My call woke Jim up. 'Is Dad all right?' 'Yes,' he replied. 'He's still in bed.' Then he said, 'He's coming, you must have woke him as well.' Father came on the phone. I found myself saying, 'I had a dream, you were dying Dad!' He could hear I was upset. He said, 'I'm all right, I'll live for years. Don't be upset, I'll live for years.' He reassured me and then wanted to know when I was coming home. 'I can't come home,' I replied. The pips were going on the phone and I had no more change.

Around about the end of October I heard Father had taken sick with a bad chest infection. Bob had called for a doctor. Father was taken into Moretonhampstead Hospital before being sent onto Exeter to run tests where they found he had cancer and a high calcium count. Father was in Exeter hospital a few days before his 73rd birthday. He was drugged up and I don't know how much he knew or not. He was asking for people, telling me the skips were ready and to order another one for the iron. I had been going up once a day as I had Clare to see to and she didn't like to be left for very long as she was still settling in at the women's refuge.

On 29 November I had a phone call from the hospital asking me to come as they felt the end was near for Father. It was about 2.10am when a nurse showed me into a small room. Father was asleep but he wasn't snoring. He always snored loudly. He was very peaceful. A nurse said she didn't think he would wake up. A friend from the refuge, Nikki, had come with me and sat very quietly in the corner. She said I shouldn't be there on my own. I had told her about my dream when we walked over. She said perhaps I'd had the dream to make it easier for when he did die.

While we were sat there a different nurse came in and started to move Father. She was rolling him onto his left side. I knew he never slept on that side because it made his shoulder hurt. He wasn't a small man, and he moaned as she pulled on him. I found myself telling the nurse to leave him alone. 'Why move him, if you don't think he will make it to the morning?' She tried telling me it was so he didn't get bedsores. I asked her to leave him in peace. The nurse left. Nikki was sat quietly, and asked if I was OK? I told her a little about the well-known Sam Harris and then we sat in silence just listening to Father's sleeping breaths. Suddenly he snorted, opened his eyes, looked at me and said, 'I'm dying Peg.' I was so taken back I said, 'What, what did you say?' They were the very same words he had said in my dream. My question must have annoyed him because he grumbled and mumbled something before going back to sleep. He died later than morning.

He had the cancer from years of chain-smoking, but pneumonia was what took him off.

Mr Small *Photograph courtesy of Peggy Harris*

MR SMALL

I met Mr Small through the refuge. He used to bring secondhand furniture for women who were moving into their new homes as most of us came to the refuge in what we stood up in and we all had to start again. He even moved us out to our new accommodation free of charge. Mr Small never took a penny from the women. He found I was able to lift furniture with no problem so he would call me when he needed a second pair of hands. Over the years I moved a fair bit of furniture. He was a man in late fifties/early sixties, a real gentleman.

When I first went out in his van to help he opened the door for me to get in. I told him I was able to open and close my own door, thank you, but he insisted. I wasn't used to this and it wasn't a one-off gesture: he would always do it.

He was a very kind man. When he came to the refuge everyone would rush and surround him calling, 'Mr Small! Mr Small!' I always thought that was his name but he was actually called Mr Morgan and his business was called Small Removals. Clare adored him. He would always stop and listen to what she had to say, and take an interest, even if she was only gibbering. He always made time for her and she knew he had a good supply of sweets and she would get him to part with them.

As the years went on I met his wife, who was a schoolteacher. They used to take Clare and her friend Amy to the pictures regularly as he loved to watch the new Disney films. They taught both girls how to swim. It was good for the girls to see that not all men in life were like their fathers.

Over the years he gave me many things for our home. I would clean cookers for him to sell. Some were minging, others not that dirty. I would clean the cookers for £5 a time, good or bad.

One time when we went to price a house clearance Clare was with us. Mr Small was playing with her pretending to be an ogre, and she ran into the bushes to hide. She stood in something: the biggest human turd ever. When she came out I could smell it, and it was nasty. She had it wedged on both shoes and smeared on her socks. They were her school shoes. It made me gag as I pulled off her shoes and peeled off her socks. I would have left them where they lay, and Mr Small asked what I was going to do. 'I'm leaving them,' I replied. He said, 'They are good shoes, you can't leave a good pair of shoes.' 'They stink! I'm not cleaning them!'

Dutifully he picked them up. 'I will clean them for you,' he said, smiling at Clare. He brought them back a few days later. Even after all that they still had a slight whiff and I put them in the bin.

Mr Small was the first kind man I had met after leaving Stinker. He didn't ask for anything, he was just a friendly person. He wanted to help us women to get our lives back on track with our children. He felt it was important that the children saw him as no threat. He was a kind gentleman. He helped me and the refuge and other people in and around Exeter. Eventually he retired and moved to Wales and has since passed away.

I SAT OUTSIDE A SHOP ALL NIGHT

Once I spent all night sat outside a Toymaster shop to get a cheap pushchair. I couldn't afford a new pushchair and I had to share the refuge one. I had seen one on sale for £5 in the window so I decided to queue all night. It was about the end of October. When I arrived around 7pm with a friend there were three women waiting already, probably since the shop closed at 5pm. It wasn't long before a few more people arrived, prepared for the cold. We all huddled together, but I didn't get much sleep. At 6am a few more turned up. At about 8.15am the staff started coming to work, ready to open for 9am. Now the queue was down the street. We had discussed what people wanted and no one wanted the pushchair. The door opened. The first ladies were taken in, and chose what they wanted. Me and my friend got the pushchair, a ride-on tractor and tricycle for a friend back in the refuge.

A TV IN OKEHAMPTON

Over the weeks in the refuge I got to know a lady called Judy, who had three boys. She had moved to Exeter due to domestic violence. She told me she'd had to give up her council house in Okehampton as she was worried about going back on her own to an empty house. She asked me if I would go with her to clear it out, and I agreed. So we caught the bus down, but the only thing was we had to stay the night. I couldn't believe my eyes – the state of the house, the dirt. By the time I had swept from upstairs down I had a quarter-full black bag of dirt. All the mattresses were pissed through, apart from one and that was the one I slept on – but I didn't take my clothes off.

Her husband started knocking on the door late in the evening, demanding the TV. It was his and he wanted it now. We had Judy's boys with us and they'd been watching the TV all evening and so we thought we'd let them do the same in the morning to keep them quiet while we finished emptying the house. Judy tried to explain to her husband that he could have the TV then. She would leave it in the shed and he could pick it up from there. He kept shouting and swearing, but after a while he went away.

I was sleeping downstairs and woke in the early hours. I could hear someone moving around the garden and tapping on the windows; it was her husband. Then there was a knocking at the front door. It was the police; they said that they had received a complaint that Judy had taken a TV. I explained to the police that it was late and the children wanted to watch it in the morning and we would leave it the back shed with all the other belongings. The policeman agreed that it was a sensible idea and we went back to bed.

I was annoyed that he had woken me up and the next morning before we left I tipped half a glass of water down the back of the TV and put it in the back shed. Judy's husband came to collect the TV and carried it to the other side of Okehampton – when he saw Judy again he said it didn't work. Serves the bugger right, keeping me up all night!

TEACH HIM A LESSON

One evening while I was staying at the refuge Marian rang and asked me to come to the pub and help her home with her friend Marlene. When I got there Marlene was well oiled, and Marian wasn't far off.

We were walking home down Longbrook Street when this young chap started following us. Marian was walking on one side of Marlene and I was holding her up on the other side. This young chap was trying to chat us up. I don't know to whom he was directing his chat-up lines but I was too busy supporting Marlene and I could hear Marian saying, 'Go away you silly little boy.' He started to say, 'I can take all three of you', and began asking who wanted it first. I said, 'If you're that desperate stick it up that,' pointing to an exhaust pipe.

This didn't deter him and he started walking backwards in front of us, up the street, still giving it all the 'old flannel'. We were nearly home and I said to Marian, 'We'd better not go in and show him where we are living because he may start hanging on the door.' So we decided to sit down on the seat just down the road. Marian was still saying, 'Go away you silly little boy'.

I sat down and lit up a cigarette. He came over to me and said he'd 'give me one'. I told him to 'piss off'. Marian was busy sorting

Marlene out. She had her back to me and Marlene was too far gone to notice; but if she'd been aware of what he was doing he would have been in trouble.

He turned and said to Marian that he could take all three of us and which one was going to go first. He then turned to me with his bits out hard as a stick and with a Union Jack hanky covering it. He came up close and I felt concerned; he was standing right in front of me, with his bits at eye level. I told him if he came any nearer I would burn him, holding the fag up. He laughed and thrust his pelvis forwards, towards me. Quietly I was panicking; I had two pissheads who weren't plugged in to what was happening. So now it was only a foot away, too close for my liking, so I stubbed my fag out on it.

He flinched and shot backwards, shouting, 'YOU BITCH!' With this I jumped up. Marian saw what I'd done and started shouting, 'GO AWAY YOU SILLY LITTLE BOY!' and took a swinging shot with her handbag, swiping him around the head. As he turned to run I kicked him up the arse and chased him across the road. He took off like a rabbit.

We often laughed about it. I wondered how he would explain it to the police if you picked him in a line up. I bet he still has a scar. Hopefully I had stopped him from attacking anyone else in the future.

ASKING FOR HELP

I didn't want my child to grow up struggling in life. I knew my limitations so I went out of my way to get people to help.

While I was at the refuge I met Margaret New who had been a teacher for children with special needs and specialised in reading. She started by helping me with the basics, but I asked her to focus on Clare. She spent hours and hours of Clare's playtime teaching her to read and write. It was difficult for Clare but Margaret persevered and by the age of four Clare was able to spell more complicated words but stumbled and blanked over the simple 'if', 'it' and 'what'. She was very persistent, and if it wasn't for Margaret's patience Clare wouldn't be able to read and write as well as she does today.

Later in life I met up with a couple I knew as a young teenager who didn't have any children of their own. She had been a teacher and he was an accountant. Together they helped Clare at weekends with her schoolwork and helped her get through her GCSEs. They were a good influence on Clare and helped her focus on her education.

Clare, Margaret (in barrow), Peggy and Amy at Margaret's home in Upton Pyne
Photograph courtesy of Peggy Harris

DEAD DEER

My friend Margaret used to take the small pre-school children from the refuge down to Sidmouth Donkey Sanctuary where they would have a ride on the donkeys. She would take three or four at a time. I would often go with her to lend a hand.

One particular day on the way home I noticed a deer had been knocked down at the side of the road. I said to Margaret that it wasn't there on the way down so it was fresh. If she turned round and picked it up I would skin it and chop it up for her and it would be free meat. She was game.

She was driving a Volvo Estate. We turned round and she pulled up level so the boot was right beside the deer. I got out of the car and could see the deer was definitely dead but only just, as it was still very warm. Opening up the back I could see the small children's faces peering over the back seat. As I lifted the deer into the boot I noticed there was blood dripping from its nostrils. There was a carrier bag lying to the side, so I put it over the deer's head to stop the blood from making a mess. The little boys started firing questions. 'What are you doing? Is it dead? Why are you putting it into the car?' I thought they would be upset if I told them it was dead and we were going to eat it, so I said we were going to take it to the vet. This seemed to satisfy them and we set off home again. Margaret entertained them by singing to them and they gradually dropped off to sleep. When we arrived at the refuge one of them mentioned the deer again and we quickly told them that we were going to take it to the vet 'now', and left.

We took the deer to Margaret's house and hung it up on a beam in the garage. I told her we needed to get the guts out and then hang it for a week at least. Margaret fetched a sharp knife, gloves and a bucket. Her daughter Mary was home and came to see what was going on. I stood looking at the carcass thinking to myself how the hell am I going to gut this? I had only ever watched my Father gut and skin rabbits. I had only ever gutted a rabbit once with Aunty Angel, and she had done most of it because I was fussing about the smell.

I knew how it should be done so I cut the stomach open. The smell was enough to knock you over so I teasingly said to Mary, 'You can pull the guts out,' thinking she would be very delicate and squeamish, but to my surprise she got stuck in up to her elbows and between the three of us we got the job done. Wrapping it in a sheet to keep the flies off we hung it high so Margaret could park her car underneath.

The following day I called down to the refuge to see some friends and the little boys spotted me and ran over, pointing, and screaming in their Birmingham accents, 'Murderer! Murderer! Murderer!' With all this commotion I had to explain to their mother what they were going on about.

OLD REG

Eventually I left the refuge and moved into a three-storey house in bedsit land. The landlady let me have a Baby Belling cooker so I could cook meals for me and Clare. For the rest of the house it was bed and breakfast. Everyone would have to be in to have a cooked meal at 5.30 in the evening.

We used to have to walk up three flights of stairs to get to the top of the house. On the top floor were two old men. One was a very fat man called Dave, who was a lollipop man, and the other was Old Reg.

Reg was a gentleman and always dressed smartly. Clare would always be out talking to him in the morning on the landing. The poor old man had trouble with his legs and found the stairs hard. He often nattered away to Clare and gave her biscuits.

Clare took to dragging him into our room in the morning to play. I would make him a cup of tea. Clare would boss him around and I would always be apologising to him. He said he didn't mind, she was the boss. She would dress him up and if he hadn't had a shave in the morning she would send him back to his room for a shave. The more I told her not to, the more he would say, 'It's all right, she's OK, she's the boss.' Clare would hear him say it was fine and so would not stop. He loved her attention.

He would come every morning for a cup of tea and bring his newspaper in and sit with Clare and ask her which horse was going to win today. Clare, not yet four, couldn't read, so she would point to a random horse and sometimes Reg would back it. Most times the horse she had picked would win or be placed and he would share his winnings with her.

He told me that he had been a soldier and he had seen action that had troubled him. He was married once and had a baby son but never saw him after he was two. He said it was entirely his fault as he would sooner live in a bottle. He'd had a drink problem for years and still suffered nightmares. When we eventually moved out, poor Old Reg was gutted. I told him I was only in the next street and we would be back to see him but he could come and see us whenever he liked. He only came once. He wasn't well, and it wasn't long after that he passed away.

Amy and Clare at Great Ley *Photograph courtesy of Peggy Harris*

TIME AT GREAT LEY

I first met Margaret when I was in the refuge; she was a plainly dressed person with a strong Catholic faith. Many of the women were sceptical and thought of her as a do-gooder. They would take advantage and leave their children with her so they could go into town. I was suffering with a bad head and felt isolated in Exeter and was looking for a friend. I tried to help her out and make her a cup of tea every now and then as I felt sorry for her, left with the children. She started up a playgroup at the refuge, and for several years took the pre-school children to the Donkey Sanctuary once a week.

SUMMERTIME 1988

After a few months our friendship grew and she invited me out to her home, Great Ley, at Upton Pyne near Exeter. She lived on an old farm with a few outbuildings, an orchard and a couple of acres. She would come and pick Clare and me up and take us out to her house, where she lived with her husband and young daughter Amy. She had two older daughters who were away at university. Amy and Clare would often play in one of the outbuildings, making huts and inventing games. Amy was three years older than Clare and was always delighted to have someone to play with.

When I first looked round the farm I couldn't help noticing there was a lot of scrap metal kicking around in the barn and outbuildings. I told Margaret that if she cleaned up the brass, copper and aluminium I would help her take it to the scrap dealer in Exeter and get her a good price. The next time I saw Margaret she told me that she had cleaned the metal and it was ready to go, but when I went and had a look at it I couldn't see any difference. I said, 'I thought you said you cleaned it.' 'Yes,' she replied, 'I came out with a bucket of water and gave it a good wash.' She made me laugh, as I had meant to clean the metal by separating it and knocking off the iron.

By this time Clare and I were living in a bedsit in Exeter. I used to love going out to Great Ley to escape from the city. Margaret was having trouble with her husband and together we found comfort in our friendship. She took me under her wing. I would try and help with odd jobs like rubbing down the window frames ready for her husband to repair. We would cook cakes together and pre-make dinners for the freezer.

Peggy waterproofing the chimney at Great Ley *Photograph courtesy of Peggy Harris*

They bought a property in Exeter for foreign students and encouraged me to move out of the bedsit I was in and rent the two ground floor rooms so I didn't have to struggle with three flights of stairs and Clare wouldn't be exposed to the odd array of people who shared the house. When I moved, I dropped down the housing list as we were less at risk. I couldn't get rehoused as the council had changed the point system without notifying me so I dropped to the bottom of the list. After a few months of living there Margaret suggested that I should buy my own place. She looked into it and helped me with the paperwork and offered to be my guarantor. I couldn't have done it without her.

During this time Margaret's marriage slowly fell apart and after 20 years together they decided to separate, which meant I started to spend a lot more time out at Great Ley.

The maintenance of Great Ley was never-ending and she found it hard to keep on top of the half-acre garden. I would help her cut the grass, pick the fruit and rotavate the garden. I remember the first time I used the rotavator. It was a petrol engine Honda and had three speeds and a reverse. I soon worked out how to start it up and put it into gear. It started to churn the ground up. I felt it was a bit slow so gave it a bit more throttle and we started to move along nicely. I was working my way around the vegetable patch. I must have lost concentration and let the pressure off the handles. The tines jumped up out of the soil, and the next thing I knew the rotavator was running along the top of the soil and onto the lawn. I hadn't noticed it had a brake and instinctively pulled back on it, shouting 'Whoa!' as I tried to stop it from running away.

Now on the grass, which was a harder surface, the machine was jumping around digging and pulling me around with it. It dragged me through a bush and ended up trying to climb a tree before I could turn it off.

Margaret grew her own veg and made her own bread and jam. Now her husband had gone she was struggling financially and so we decided to try and live off the land to reduce costs. We went to the market and bought up a mixed batch of chickens for laying. We bought up most of the cheap lots. The kids were always incredibly noisy and excited by these outings. Once we came across a large Henry hoover vacuum box with a red washing basket tied down with cord with a very indignant male gander inside. He was making such a racket that most of the customers were giving him a wide berth as they thought he was trouble. We bought him as he was going cheap. The kids named him Honkey which was in keeping with his character. He would bully the chickens and catch the cat by the tail and refuse to let go. The cat would ignore him and determinedly continue to walk on the spot until he did! Always very proud of himself he would flap his wings and honk softly as if he was laughing. After a few weeks we found him a mate, Snowy, which helped settle him down.

As meat was so expensive we decided to get some part-grown fattening chickens from one of my uncles. We would have 10 or 20 at a time. When they were ready I would kill and pluck them. Margaret would freeze most of hers, selling one or two to cover the cost of the feed, and I would sell mine. I remember when I got the first lot of chickens I knew I could kill and pluck them but I didn't know how to draw them. When my father used to draw them, they always stank and the smell would make me feel sick. Margaret's neighbour Phyllis used to draw chickens years ago so

I asked her if she could show me how to do it. She showed me a couple of times until I was well on my way. I have drawn hundreds since, mainly turkeys.

I suggested getting a pig for the winter. We got a little pig, the runt of the litter, which the kids called Pinkie. The farmer gave us some pig food with dried milk in it. The pig wasn't much bigger than the cat to begin with. The cat took a liking to the pig food and spent a lot of time eating and sleeping in with the pig. One evening I was watching them eating. Pinkie had grown a few sizes and had started to act a bit more like a pig and pushed the cat out of the way roughly with his snout. The cat was not having that and attacked the pig's ear. With teeth and claws the cat brought the pig down to his knees, grunting softly. Poor Pinkie had to stand back and let the cat take first pickings.

We were good friends for many years and had lots of fun and laughs. Eventually Margaret remarried and moved away. I will not forget how much she helped us. She gave me freedom and steered me on a path so I could be a better mother. She helped me to learn the basics of reading and writing and helped my daughter with her learning difficulties. She helped me get a home and – most importantly – she gave me friendship when I needed it most.

FUN AND GAMES

I used to tell Clare and Amy stories about how my brothers and I grew up in the scrapyard and how we had our adventures. Even though life on a scrapyard could be hard, when I was little I just saw it as a giant playground. I wanted the girls to share some of the adventures I had growing up, but I didn't teach them the dangerous games.

Margaret and I always encouraged the girls to play and use their imagination instead of sitting in front of the television. On sunny days they would be out in the outbuildings or in the hedges making huts, running around, climbing trees and inventing games. On rainy days they would be indoors playing dress up and directing their own plays.

One summer we cleared the top shippen, a large barn at the top of the garden, so they could play outside all year round. I hung a swing from one of the beams and made an indoor swing ball by welding the pole to an old mini wheel so it was mobile and could be played in or outdoors. I made netball hoops from scrap metal, a high jump out of bamboo sticks for the girls to practise on and I eventually found a basketball hoop at the scrapyard which I brought back for them, amongst many other things.

In the outbuildings there was plenty of wood and an old-fashioned pram. I decided to surprise the girls with a go-kart. I set about sawing and hammering bits of wood together and took the wheels from the pram to make a very rustic go-kart. The delighted girls spent many hours pulling the cart up to the top of yard and taking it in turns whizzing down the slope.

Another day I saw that they had tried to make their own bows and arrows but had not succeeded. I got a little carried away as I set about making them a set each, and made arrows with bird feathers to help give them more flight. Before I handed them over I thought I would have a little play to see what they were like. I got the girls to set up a few cardboard boxes on the lawn and was amazed to see the arrow go

Clare and the go-kart Peggy made for her *Photograph Peggy Harris*

straight through! They even stuck into wood! Clare was excited and thought she was going to have a go but I slackened off the bows and gave them bent sticks as I was afraid they would shoot each other.

It was a hot summer in 1995. I went to Bob's to see if I could get an inner tube so the girls could play in the river. Bob could only find an old lorry wheel and tyre. What a job to get the tube out! We didn't have any machine to press the tyre off, just a tyre lever, a sledgehammer and brute force.

The tube blew up into a huge ring. I made a seat and two paddles out of scrap wood and squeezed it into the car. Margaret and I and the two girls bundled in and went down to Brampford Speke. We had many hours of fun splashing and jumping into the river.

Peggy, Clare and Amy celebrating Clares birthday

MARGARET'S MINI

When Margaret's husband left, he gave her the house but wanted his car (she had the use of it until the settlement was completed). I was looking for a cheap car as she didn't have much money. I was out helping Bob picking up scrap at a garage in Chagford and noticed a little blue Mini parked in the corner, with no seats or carpet. I asked the owner if it was scrap. He said make him an offer; I looked it over as he said it was a runner. It didn't look like it was as it was rusted out, so I offered him £10 because that's what it would have been worth for scrap. Bob was still trading in cars so I knew I would be able to get plenty of parts. I worked on it for a month doing it up before I gave it to her. It was a bit of a comedown from a Volvo Estate but she was over the moon with it and ran it for three or four years. I kept it on the road with the help of six different Minis, and Bob's help too.

NOEL

It was odd, really, Margaret had gone to London on a course and met a very young man called Noel. She had shown him pictures of her daughters and he had taken a liking to one. I am not sure of the arrangements, but somehow he had arrived in Devon.

Clare and I had him to stay at our place, as it was Margaret's property and her daughter wasn't interested in him. So he sat and talked to us for most of the weekend. In one of his conversations he told us how he was going to work in the oil industry in Dubai to make his fortune. During that weekend he tried to give me advice about changing my life and getting out and doing more. He knew I could drive, he knew I had come from the scrapyard and that I hadn't seen my family for a few years, and he knew I couldn't afford a car.

Noel had come down on the train but at home he had an old Mark III Ford Escort which he wanted to get rid of. He didn't want anything for it but he didn't want to leave it at home as he was afraid his younger brother would try to drive it. So he announced that he was going to give Clare the car. She was only five at the time but he told her that it was her car and that Mummy would take her out in it! Clare was really chuffed.

About a week later he turned up with the red Escort. It had a small problem – a wheel cylinder had gone in the brakes – but he had taxed it and put a year's insurance on it.

He was a very generous young man. He gave us this car to improve our lives and it did. He gave us freedom as it enabled us to go out, to visit family and friends – and he helped me to get where I am today.

I kept the car going for several years, a lot longer that it should have. This young man's kindness and generosity was the big stepping-stone in my life. When he knew us we had nothing, but since then I have made a home, got work and regained my independence. He wisely told me to get myself some education. I've never forgotten him.

THE DAY I WENT BACK TO THE YARD

I'd had the MkIII Ford Escort a few weeks before I decided to go back to the yard. It felt strange driving down the lane I hadn't seen for a few years, and knowing Father wasn't at the yard any more. Nothing had changed much; it was still full of scrap.

I felt like a stranger. Clare was firing a hundred and one questions, eager to get out of the car and have a look round. I was nervous, my heart going ten to the dozen. Getting out of the car I told Clare to stick close to me – and absolutely no running.

When we arrived Bob was out but Jim was there. Jim informed me that Stinker was still working there and that he and Bob were out in the truck. It was getting dimpsy as the night was pulling in. Before I knew it they were back. I was so scared that he would see us and confront us as I still had strong memories of what he had done to me and had only just started to get over the pain he had inflicted. We hid in a caravan, despite Clare's efforts to snoop and investigate. It was a short visit; we left as soon as the coast was clear, after finding out that Stinker didn't work on Sundays.

Eventually I went back again on my own and met Bob. He was very prickly due to what had happened in the past. But he only had one side of the story and it was only now that I could tell him what had really happened, and that Stinker's long-term plan was to take over the yard.

The last time I had seen Bob we had fallen out over something trivial. He had asked me to carry a battery in the truck so it could charge up as we drove along. I was out working with Stinker all day and he must have knocked the crocodile clip off so the battery didn't charge (it was in his footwell).

Bob was annoyed with me as he thought I had deliberately not listened to him. It kicked off into a slanging match. We fought viciously like two children. I hurt him maliciously with my words so he bent my thumb back, causing me severe pain; I thought he had broken it. As he stepped back I high-kicked him in the face, cutting his cheek. We fought for blood; it was nothing to be proud of. He chased me out of the back door. I grabbed an old jam jar that was full of mud and heaved it at him full pelt. As it flew he closed the door so I would miss, but it went straight through the pane of glass. What he didn't know was that Stinker had been digging at me all day and I was wound up already. It was the last straw being accused of something I hadn't done. In a moment of rage I foolishly shouted, 'You have no right to hurt me. I'll report you to the police, if you ever hurt me again.'

Stinker, who was sat quietly watching the entire scene, did nothing. He could have defused the situation but chose not to. I pleaded with him to tell Bob that I hadn't done it, but he did nothing. When I came back in, Bob had slunk off to his caravan with wounded pride. Stinker quietly but severely told me, 'You threatened it, you follow through with it. Else you'll get a bigger beating than what you had now.' I didn't want to. It was a foolish threat, I hadn't meant it. He was my twin.

I am so ashamed. I had to call the police, and a big burly policeman turned up. I was the first to rush up to him. 'Don't arrest him, just warn him,' I pleaded. I said it so Stinker couldn't hear.

On the journey home Stinker continued being forceful. He told me not talk to Bob in the morning; I didn't speak to him for the rest of the week. The next day when I went over to the yard I thought Bob would still be in bed, but he was up early and came over to see me as if nothing was wrong. I had a lump in my throat and could see it hurt him; it hurt me too. I had to ignore him. Stinker didn't stop there; for the rest of the week he dictated what I should do and say.

The following Tuesday at five o'clock I was sat in the car wanting to go home. Stinker and my brothers were talking to a customer in front of my car, and the customer leaned against my bonnet. Eventually Stinker got in the car so we could go home. Randomly he started accusing me of fancying the young chap who'd sat on my car. I didn't fancy him. It escalated out of control as he interrogated me. Every time I denied it, I received a slap and he grew angrier and angrier. The slaps turned into a thump, a back hander. Apparently I should have got out and told the man to get off my car but I didn't see the problem with him leaning on it.

Over five miles or so of country lanes he repeatedly asked the same question and got the same response. I was trapped in a small Mini. I knew tonight was my beating; he wasn't going to let up. He would smack my head into the steering wheel as I drove along and then lay into me because I swerved. I couldn't do anything right. He started to say I was disgusting to do what I did to my own brother, thumping me repeatedly. I pulled out onto the main road at Venton Straight. An articulated lorry was coming down the opposite direction. I was in two minds about putting us under the lorry. Kill him, kill myself – it would all stop – I knew what was coming. I got so close, but I let the lorry pass.

I turned onto the Iddesleigh road. There is a pull in, a bit of lane. He told me to stop there. He rolled a cigarette. I sat quiet, still said nothing, scared. He started questioning, over and over again, the same questions. He grabbed my hair and pulled my head back, stubbing his cigarette out into my eye. I had luckily closed my eyes, so he just burned my eyelid before he rammed my head down into the steering wheel.

This seemed to go on for hours, but eventually we arrived home. I thought it would stop there, but when we entered the house he said to Number Two, 'What do you think about this?' and proceeded to tell her what was in his head. He asked her to fetch an electric cable. She knew what that meant as she had received that electric treatment herself many years before. Luckily for me she pretended she couldn't find a cable. Instead she brought in a cold dinner.

I didn't want to eat, I didn't want anything. He made me eat the cold dinner: cold chips, cold beans and cold fish fingers. I wasn't to move until I had finished it. Clare was looking on, worried. She could sense something was wrong, and as soon as I had finished she climbed up onto my lap. He asked Number Two if he should give me another hiding. She had to answer, 'If you want to.' He told her to remove Clare from my lap and to take her to the other room. Clare started screaming; she didn't want to go. When they had left the room, it was quiet. He pinned me into an old armchair. He stood in front of me asking the same questions and, not receiving the answers he wanted, proceeded to beat me. I was so scared I couldn't cry.

He pounded me in the arm with his fist. I was left bruised from my shoulder to my elbow for three months. He held the side of my face and slapped me as hard as he could with the other so I would feel the full impact. When his hand hurt he accused me of causing it and changed to the other, hitting me harder. He was annoyed I wasn't crying but I couldn't. I was stunned. I wasn't me. I was numbed. I was a shell.

Because I didn't cry, couldn't cry, he didn't stop until I pretended by making weeping noises. When I whimpered he backed off. He then demanded that I drive him home to Number Three's house.

During the beating he coldly and collectedly told me that if I left I couldn't take the baby and that if I did he would instruct Social Services and have the baby taken off me for being an unfit mother. I was young, I knew no difference and I believed his words. He barked at me that if I dared to leave I would have to be a million miles away as he would find me and put me down a mineshaft. He said he would kill us both and tell everyone we had just f****d off. I shall never forget what he threatened me during that beating.

The next day I thought he would be all right. Usually he would carry on as if nothing had happened, but he was still cold. You could cut the atmosphere with a knife. I didn't dare move or do anything out of place in case he would strike. I made sure I didn't put a foot wrong driving. When we got to the yard Father was out feeding the chickens. Stinker got out as if nothing was wrong, 'Hello Sam, you all right?' I sat for a few moments, not knowing what to do. I couldn't face my father; my face was a different shade, disfigured. I got out of the car and headed down the lane and sat on a big rock. I couldn't tell Dad, I was ashamed.

There was a voice in my head – 'You have to get out now Peggy, you have to go.' But how, how was I going to go… and where was I going to go?

As I walked back to up the lane I decided I was going to get out, I had to get out. Approaching the car, I needed an excuse to leave. Picking up an empty gas cylinder, I put it on my shoulder so Father couldn't see my face. I shouted out, 'I'm going to change the gas cylinder and go to the bank.'

I got in the car, turned round and started going up the lane. My head began to rush, where shall I go? I looked across the seat and saw Stinker's lunch bag. I found myself turning round and putting it in the house. I don't know why I did it, I just did.

I had to start up again, drive up the lane. By this time my legs were jelly, I wasn't calm and collected, I was all over place, I was a mess. I got into Chagford and dropped the cylinder off and put the money in the bank. I went to my Nan's. She hadn't seen me for several weeks, as Stinker had banned me from seeing them and letting them see the baby.

I let myself in the back kitchen door. Nan was in the front room. To start with she didn't recognise me. Nan was in her late eighties and as she got closer she realised it was me and my face was bruised and swollen. She put her hands onto my face, and I just broke down. All I kept saying was, 'I've got to get a million miles away, he's going to kill us.' She held me in her arms. Angel, my aunt, was also there. Sitting me down, Nan told Angel that she would have to help me. All I remember was that Angel had been on the phone and she was given the numbers of two refuges, one in Torquay and other one Exeter. I knew the code for Exeter, so she rang Exeter. They had a vacancy, a free room if I could get there. Angel took the address and then we had to get Clare. I wasn't going to leave my baby behind.

Clare was out at Iddesleigh. Angel, my other aunt Cherry (who decided to come and help) and I headed over there. I was nervous and afraid that he would ring through and warn Number Two not to let me in. I had made arrangements with Aunty to park at the top of the lane for ten minutes which would allow me to run down and get into the house, without causing suspicion as I would make up some excuse. As I ran I noticed that the Jehovah's Witnesses were just leaving, as they were backing out into the lane. I didn't want them to see me, as they would stay longer. So I jumped over a gate and hid behind a hedge.

When they eventually went by I climbed back into the lane and ran down to the house, knocked on the door and pushed in past as Number Two opened it. 'I've got a flat tyre up the road, I need the loo and need to make a phone call.' Number Two said she'd put the kettle on. Whilst she was busy I pulled out a suitcase full of our personal belongings, birth certificates and bank book. No clothes. No shoes. I didn't think like that.

Just before I came down the stairs, Aunty Angel knocked on the door and asked to see Clare. The story had been arranged that Nan hadn't seen Clare for so long that she wanted to see her. By this time Aunty Angel had picked Clare up into her arms. I walked down the stairs with my suitcase. As I got to the foot of the stairs Number Two called out, 'Your tea is here and Aunty wants to take Clare.' With that I walked out of the door and said 'Thank you, bye,' and kept going.

We all bundled into the car as fast as we could. Aunty Angel was nervous as we headed off to Exeter. Aunty Cherry held Clare on her lap in the back. I was anxious as I was headed to somewhere I didn't know, knowing I was to start a new life. Clare sat oblivious and happy.

When we arrived at the house in Exeter I opened the door and went in. The aunties didn't come in; they were anxious to get back to Nan's in case Stinker had gone looking for me there. Clare stuck to me like glue as we met the people who were going to help us start our new lives.

To start with Bob didn't want to know but as I talked to him, telling him what had really happened, he could relate to it as he had experienced and witnessed some of Stinker's behaviour himself. It was a while before we were on an even keel again, but time has been a great healer. And Clare helped to break the ice, as Bob enjoyed playing with her as she grew up.

JIM RIPPED ME OFF BUT I GOT MY OWN BACK

Jim is my eldest brother. In 1992 Noel's red MkIII Ford Escort needed a new pair of wings to replace its rusty ones. I asked Jim if he would cut the wings off an old scrap Escort that my brother Bob had and weld them on mine. He said he would and that it would cost me £40 to put them on and spray them. It seemed a reasonable deal, so I left the car with him.

He bought the car back after a week but he'd only done one wing. He still wanted his £40 and I had no choice but to pay up even though it wasn't such a good deal any more. Then when I came to drive the car I noticed that he had even used the tank of petrol that I'd put in. He left me feeling cheated and bitter, but there wasn't anything I could do about it.

About a year later, Margaret and I called in to see Bob, my twin, and I noticed Jim unloading his three-wheeler. In one hand he had an old picture and I asked him what he was going to do with it. He said he was throwing it on the fire. He had been clearing out an old lady's garage and this was the last load. I said, 'That looks old! I'll take it to the antique dealer and see if it's worth anything.' He handed it over. It was an old oil painting of a valley somewhere on the moor, painted in late evening. The picture had been damaged by water running down it and seemed dark and dull. It had a big ornate gold frame that was flaking and dirty.

I put the picture in the car and on the way back to Exeter decided to call in at Phillips the auctioneers to see if it was worth anything. I lifted it out of the car by the wire on the back of the frame, started to cross the road and the wire snapped. The picture crashed to the ground and the frame broke off in big pieces. I turned to Margaret and said, 'That's buggered it now!' But she said, 'You might as well go and see what it would have been worth now you're here.' I took it into the auction house, embarrassed by such a shabby picture. This chap came over and had a good look and said he had sold one like it a couple of months ago and it had made £300, but as this one was damaged it would only make, at best, £60. I said, 'Take it, £60 is £60!' Then I remembered being stitched up the year before over the car wings. I thought, 'If Jim asks me if it was worth anything I'll tell him how I dropped it and leave it at that.'

Six weeks passed and I forgot that Phillips had the picture. One morning a letter arrived for me with a cheque enclosed for £360. I couldn't believe it. That old picture made so much! I decided I wouldn't tell Jim how much it made or even that I had sold it. He had me for £40 and I had £360. I took the money and bought myself a Mig welder. I taught myself to weld and put on my own wing!

CHARLIE PIG

Margaret and I had filled up the freezer with our chickens and we thought it would be nice to have a change. As the autumn was coming on we decided it would be ideal to raise a pig for the winter. Over the years we had done four pigs, but I remember Charlie Pig the most.

We bought a runt pig and the children decided to call him Charlie. Charlie was a very friendly Large White cross Berkshire pig. The children spent a lot of time playing with him. They would tickle his belly and he would drop to the floor so they could scratch him all over with a broom. They could put a rope round his neck and he would take them for a walk around the orchard. Clare used to sit on his back as he pottered round the yard. We were all very fond of Charlie.

It was especially hard when the day came that I had to walk up to the top shed. The children knew he was for the freezer but had pleaded for days beforehand to keep him as a pet. I found he was the hardest pig I'd ever have to kill but we had him for one reason and that was for meat. The children were at school when Margaret and I put the water on to boil, which would help us remove the pig's hair; we hung up the pulley and blocks. It was time.

I hadn't fed Charlie that morning. He followed me eagerly up to and into the shed, sniffling and snuffling the floor as I rattled the food bucket. I put a little food on the floor where I wanted him to stand. Margaret went out of the door after handing me the single-barrel shotgun. I gave Charlie a little scratch behind the ear with the end of the barrel. He grunted softly and lay down, ready for me to tickle his belly. My heart started to race, feeling guilty; he was a sweet-natured pig. It was a shame to kill him, but that's what we had him for.

So, still giving him a scratch behind his ear, I pulled the trigger gently. That was the end of Charlie.

Margaret came in to put the boiling water into the bath ready to dip the carcass so we could scrape and remove the thick hair. She touched my arm and quietly said, 'Well done,' knowing that it was hard for me to do. We worked quietly and swiftly as now he was dead, he was just meat. It was a big rush to cut the throat and get the body up into the air. Hitching the back legs to the pulley blocks I hung him up while the carcass twitched and the blood drained into a bucket.

Peggy and Amy making a snowman in the garden at Great Ley *Photograph courtesy of Peggy Harris*

It was a few Sundays before we had roast pork but when we did, the first thing the girls asked was, 'Is this Charlie?' as they looked glumly at their plates. This continued for several months – every time there was pork on the plate.

CLARE AND THE CHICKEN

One time we had roast chicken for Sunday dinner, and then went out visiting friends. I had left the chicken out on the side to cool down. That evening when we got back I noticed it had been picked at, and it was only Clare and me in the house. I knew I hadn't picked at it so it must have been my daughter. So I told her off for picking at the carcass as it was for next day's tea. She denied picking at it. I told her it must be her and she was to stop lying. I sent her to bed.

I made tea with the leftovers for the next evening. A week went by and we had chicken again for Sunday dinner and again we went out. That evening we came home and I walked into the dark kitchen, but before I could put the light on there was a thud and something ran into my leg that made me shout out. Clare put the light on and there was a cat. We didn't have a cat; it was someone else's cat that had come in through the old cat flap in the window.

Clare stood there and said: 'I told you I didn't pick at the chicken!' Then I had to apologise to her.

CURIOSITY KILLS THE CAT

Margaret put half a dozen eggs from our chickens under a broody hen. The hen sat on them for more than three weeks and came out with only two chicks. Amy and Clare wanted to know what was wrong with the other eggs. I knew they would be bad, but these children had never seen a bad egg before. I told them to open one knowing full well that it would go pop, and make a stink. They took the eggs and went to open one. 'Pop!' it went and they went running off, coughing and spluttering. You know what it is with kids: curiosity kills the cat!

I STOPPED THE TRAIN

My 25th birthday present from Margaret was a trip to Paris. Clare was looked after by her elder daughter at Great Ley. I had never been out of Britain before and I had never flown. We caught a train to Bristol and a bus to the airport, and then got on a small plane to Paris. All OK so far. I was a little nervous as the plane gathered speed down the runway, then all of a sudden me legs were coming up and I was tipped back in my seat. It made me shout out, 'Oh, shit,' and I got told off by Margaret because she was embarrassed. She took it upon herself to tell people it was my first flight and to excuse my language!

We had a good five days' exploring Paris, going on the Metro to Versailles then walking around the palace and gardens for a day. We took a boat down the Seine, past Notre Dame, and afterwards we went to the Louvre. After five days of walking I was looking forward to going home. On the way back we decided to spend all the rest of our francs in the airport. I spent mine on coffee. Then it was time to get on the plane.

Just before boarding I said to Margaret, 'I need the toilet.' She said, 'Wait until you get on the plane.' We found our seats and Margaret said, 'Wait until we are up and then ask the steward.' We were in the air and the steward came over and I asked, 'Where's the toilet, please?' The steward replied, 'There is no toilet on this flight. As it is a short flight, you have to wait until we land.' I thought that was all right as I wasn't desperate.

We landed in Bristol, gathered up our bags and I headed for the toilet but Margaret said, 'You can't go, the bus is waiting, quick – if we miss it we'll miss the train too. Wait until you are on the train.' So we rushed to get on the bus but I was starting to suffer now: I needed to go. We arrived at the train station after running from the bus stop, and just as we got there the tannoy announced that our train was leaving. We raced down the platform to see it starting to pull off. Margaret said, 'We have missed it, we will have to wait an hour.' 'Good,' I said, 'where's the toilet?' I was looking round for the signs when the conductor came up and asked which station we needed. 'Exeter,' we said. He then said, pointing at the train that was just pulling in, 'This train will stop in Exeter. It's the milk train, it will take a little longer but it's better than waiting here for the next train.' 'All right,' said Margaret, picking up her bags. I said, 'I need the toilet, Margaret.' She said, 'Wait until you are on the train.'

We piled onto the train, but it was so crowded there wasn't anywhere to sit. We had to wait for several stops before we managed to get a seat, and then the ticket collector came for our tickets. I asked him if there was a toilet on the train. He said that there were none as it was a short train and I would have to wait till I got to Exeter. This was the first station the train stopped at which had a toilet.

I told the conductor I was desperate and had been waiting to go since Paris and I was in agony. He said, 'I will see if we can do an unscheduled stop.' Soon, a voice came over the speakers saying, 'Due to a passenger needing the toilet we will be stopping at the next station.' Everyone was looking and I had to get up and leave the train, run along the platform, up and over the bridge to the deserted platform on the other side. I found the toilet but when I got there I had been waiting so long that I couldn't go! There was a train full of people waiting too.

When I came out of the toilet, everyone was cheering and clapping. I was so embarrassed – but very relieved!

Runaway pony

I had an Exmoor pony on loan from a friend called Pat Gibson. I had known Pat for years; she'd given me a pony, Storm, to break to ride when I was 14. Now I was grown up with a daughter of my own. In the summer of 1995 Pat lent me a pony called Friday; he was a six-year-old Exmoor. He was a little green and she hoped I would bring him on. Clare was eight at the time and I was using Margaret's field and courtyard out at Upton Pyne. Margaret's daughter Amy was 11 and was very keen on riding. I would go out with them most days. I would ride a pushbike and Amy and Clare would take it in turns to ride Friday and the bike.

Friday was very good in traffic but he was scared of tractors, as one had frightened him once. So I would ride him out to find tractors. As it was a farming area, there were lots about. I would make him stand and watch the tractors working the fields. In the evenings they were left parked up so I would ride Friday up to the tractors and let him smell them. Amy and Clare would ride him round them until he wasn't bothered by them any more, even when meeting them in the road.

Friday was very good with us riding around him on our bicycles, but he would jump if someone came rushing down a hill on a mountain bike. They are silent but when the brakes are applied they make a squealing noise. This would make Friday panic.

Amy and Clare could do anything with Friday. They'd dress him up and build handy pony courses, making him walk over plastic sacks, carrying water and moving things around on him. They would jump him and I taught them how to do gymkhana games and Friday loved it. But he didn't like long sticks; he would get very upset if you picked up a long stick. So when he saw people going fishing with rods he would rush past. Somewhere in his life it was obvious someone had used a long stick on him.

We used to ride around the lanes and in and out of the villages like Brampford Speke, Thorverton and Newton St Cyres. Our rides would depend on how fit I was feeling on the day or how hot or wet it was. On this particular day we were going to ride around Brampford Speke. Amy was going to ride the first half and Clare would ride home.

Clare and Amy had swapped over at the top of the village. We had just got to the bottom of the hill when I heard Amy shout, 'Bicycles!' I told Clare to ride Friday into a gateway so he would be off the road. There were about six boys on mountain bikes with fishing rods sticking out the back of them. The brakes squealed as they tried to slow, and Friday took one look and panicked. I couldn't get off my bike in time; I grabbed his bridle as he lunged forwards. I tried to hold him but he pushed me across the road, still straddled across the bike. The boys were whooshing around us. Friday jumped sideways, catching his bit in the handlebars. Lifting the bike up he tipped me over, knocking me to the ground. I remember seeing his hooves and belly going over me. Clare was shouting, and I could hear the squealing bike brakes. The boys were on their way back to see what was happening.

Friday went and stood in the gateway on the other side of the road. I could see Clare was still on him, and she was crying. I tried to get up from under my bike quietly, trying not to scare him. I saw he had broken his bit. Clare hadn't noticed that she suddenly had no brakes.

We rode Friday in a Pelham bit, which has a curb chain that goes under the chin. This chain was against Friday's neck. As I got up a boy came towards me saying, 'It wasn't our fault.' Friday must have thought that the boy was coming back for him and he wasn't going to hang around. He turned and decided to trot home. I tried to chase after him but the hill was too steep and he wasn't going to stop. It was at this point that Clare realised he didn't have a bit, and she started to panic. I could still hear the boy shouting, 'It's not our fault!' I shouted, 'Clear off!!' I knew it wasn't their fault, but he wasn't helping.

Amy was a faster runner than I was but even she couldn't catch up on that steep hill. As I reached Amy I told her to get our bikes as they were still in the middle of the road. I kept Friday in sight and shouted to Clare that she'd be all right and to keep talking to Friday as I could see that she was soon going to be out of sight.

I could hear a car coming up the hill behind. I stood in the middle of road until they stopped. Breathlessly I informed the driver that I had a runaway pony with an eight-year-old girl on his back with a broken bridle, while I opened the back door and slid in beside some elderly people. They sat stunned. 'Drive,' I ordered. They were shocked as I didn't know them and they didn't know me. It was only a short journey but I managed to tell them that the pony had panicked with the boys and the fishing rods. They said

Peggy with Clare on Friday in 1995 *Photograph courtesy of Peggy Harris*

that they had just passed them and that they had seen a bike in the middle of the road at the bottom of the hill.

We soon came across Clare and Friday in a gateway, with some people holding the pony. Clare was pointing at me saying, 'That's my Mum.' I thanked the driver for giving me a lift. Clare told me how she had shouted at the people to stop Friday. You could see that they had never held a pony before as they were holding the bridle by his ear. Friday was trying to get close to them for reassurance. I thanked them, tied the reins to the noseband and put Clare up on his back. We started to head down the hill to fetch Amy, who was nearly halfway up, struggling to push both bikes. She was looking worried but broke into a big smile when she saw us coming and could see that Friday and Clare were OK.

We headed home for tea and Amy and Clare talked about what happened for days, and how brave Clare was. This never put the girls off riding; they enjoyed Friday to the end of the summer until he went home. He was sold the following spring and went on to make other children happy.

HAND ON FIRE

We had some other adventures during the summer that Friday was with us at Great Ley.

One lunchtime I decided to lunge him for a bit of exercise. Everything was going well. He trotted nicely one way and then nicely on the other rein. Then all of a sudden something frightened him. I think it might have been cat in the hedge.

He took off in a straight a line. I thought I would be able to hold him but it happened so fast he'd pulled the rope through my hands; it was like my hands were on fire. I just had to let him go and then catch him after he had taken himself back to the courtyard. After I'd re-caught him, I had to run a bucket of cold water to cool my hands down. My right hand was worse; it was like I had put it into a fire. I knew I had to lunge him again just to finish on a good note, but I didn't know what to do with my hand as I was in so much pain. Luckily the pony co-operated and let me lunge him. After we'd finished I turned him out.

I went and raided the freezer for something cold to take the heat out and found some frozen peas. It felt good but my hand was so hot it defrosted the peas in no time at all. All that was left were some bags of homegrown broad beans. If I hadn't needed to go out that

91

afternoon I would have kept my hand in a bucket of cold water; but it was Clare's sports day and she was looking forward to me coming.

I dug my hand into several pounds of frozen broad beans and wrapped it up in a towel, then disguised it all inside a bag. Then I set off to watch the sports day. It was a nice warm afternoon. My hand was still burning; half an hour later I could feel the beans defrosting.

I was sat with all the mums and dads watching the sports when I could smell something funny, a bit like rotting vegetables. Now my hand had started throbbing. It was getting hotter and it was starting to really hurt and the smell was getting worse… the people next to me and nearby could smell it too.

The smell was getting stronger, my hand was giving me hell, and it felt like it was in hot soup. Then I realised where the smell was coming from. It was me – I had defrosted the beans and now I was cooking them. The people around me gradually started to leave their seats, and even I couldn't stick it.

I threw the beans away; I didn't fancy eating them. Clare won her races and I spent the evening with my hand in a bucket of water. The heat in my hand was so great it even warmed up the water; I had to change it several times. I had to sleep with my arm hung over the side of the bed with my hand in a bucket all night. It worked; it was better by the morning.

SNAILS AT GREAT LEY

Margaret worked hard on planting her vegetable garden. She had trouble one year with the snails eating stuff so she suggested to Amy and Clare that they could earn a few pennies by collecting snails. The girls spent not only hours but days hunting out all the snails around Great Ley. They turned over plant pots, lifted up the ivy and looked under every stone they could find. The girls weren't squeamish. They took great pleasure crunching them up with their feet and feeding them to the chickens.

Every day they would come indoors with hundreds of snails in their buckets. Margaret

92

thought they would only find a few hundred but in the end it was more like thousands. It cost Margaret a fortune!

BBC TURKEY INTERVIEW

I have plucked turkeys for years at the Malseeds' farm at Frenchbeer, near Chagford. In the old days we would start plucking from eight in the morning, and sometimes we would pluck till eight at night. The days felt very long and hard to start with. People would have lots to say at first, laughing and joking, but as time went by there was less said and just the radio playing. All you could hear was the plucking of the feathers, like a ripping noise. The door would swing

Peggy plucking turkeys at Frenchbeer in 2004

open as someone came in to collect the plucked turkeys and carry them off across the yard to be weighed and hung up.

One year a lady from BBC Radio Devon came to talk to the farmer about his turkeys. She came into the plucking house which was an old stable, its walls now covered with black plastic and the straw bales and the floor several inches deep in smelly feathers. She stood in the doorway, and watched. She asked questions but no one really wanted to talk to her. I said, 'If you want to talk about plucking turkeys you need to pluck one yourself, so you know what you are talking about.' I explained to her that she needed to pluck the wings first as they go cold the quickest and then it would be harder to remove the feathers. She half-heartedly picked at a few feathers as she asked questions.

She asked whether I was having a turkey for Christmas. I replied, 'I'm afraid not,' and she was surprised by my answer. 'Afraid not?' 'Yes,' I said, 'After plucking it and looking up its arse for a fortnight I don't fancy eating it!' A roar of laughter went up. A few days later she played it on the morning radio for the whole county to hear.

LICE

One year at Frenchbeer we had 3000 turkeys to pluck for Christmas. Everything was going well, but then one day I noticed that the birds had livestock running on them. The more you plucked the more the lice gathered together and then ran up your arms. They would sit under your collar and crawl around your body. They made me itch madly. Roy, my friend, who also plucked, said I was just making a fuss. I told him, 'Wait till they get on you and see how long you can stick them.' I told him they like nooks and crannies and warm places and to have a good look when he was in the bath.

Next day Roy said, 'You're right, they were under me collar and in other places!' The farmer thought we were just making a fuss but produced some louse powder, which I tipped down the front and back of me trousers and down me neck. The little buggers was running everywhere. They were running up your legs from out of the feathers on the floor. In the end we all had a good delousing. The stable was deloused as well and we managed to finish plucking.

Previously I used to fatten chickens myself, at Margaret's place at Upton Pyne. We raised chickens for the freezer, plus she sold some to cover the cost of buying and feeding them. One day I was out preparing the chickens; I would hang them in the doorway of the barn to pluck them. Then I noticed they had lice.

The cat came and sat on the windowsill, where he often sat and watched me pluck. He knew he would get some titbits after they were drawn, but this day the cat was impatient: he put his paw around the window to try and snatch the chicken. I would push the cat off the windowsill, but when he came back again he annoyed me. I thought I'll annoy you, you little bugger, so I picked up some lice off the chicken and put them on his back. He didn't notice them for a while and just carried on trying to get the chicken. Then all of a sudden he felt them; they'd started to move and wriggle. His coat started to twitch; he was trying to ignore the tickling feeling. He was purring and making eyes at me for the chicken, rubbing against the window, stretching out his paw and meowing. Then all of a sudden he started to scratch, left leg, then right leg. The window ledge was too small to take his wriggling and he toppled off and landed on all fours. He just couldn't stand it; he was scratching his left side, and then his right side, and I laughed and laughed. I could hardly see to pluck the chicken.

I wasn't worried about the cat with the lice because I knew he'd probably be able scratch them off – they were as big as a match head!

Portrait of Peggy Harris, 2014

A MOTHER'S WORST NIGHTMARE

The day that Clare got attacked was 18 June 2000. It was a Sunday, Father's Day, the hottest day of the year. I have a very clear memory of it: an ordinary day which turned into a nightmare.

We were visiting Bob at the scrapyard. I was going to work on a car to get it through its MOT, and we had dinner down at Mother's. Bob had let Clare have a pushbike. I wasn't too pleased that she was riding it around the block but Bob had said I was to let her grow up and let go of the apron strings. My concern was that she would get knocked off her bike as some people drive like idiots in the lanes. As kids we used to roam around the area. It was the safest place in the world when we were growing up. I would often let Clare go the quarter mile down the lane to the brook to paddle, and ride her bike up and down the lane.

I was changing the brakes on my car and had gone further down the yard to a scrapped car for some spares. I hadn't seen Clare for a while and was a little worried so I'd asked Bob if he'd seen her. He said he had and that she was all right. She had gone down to Mother's. (He hadn't told me that he had wound her up, teasing her that I had gone home without her; and I only found out later that Mother had told her she was asleep, and so

Clare had gone back to the brook again.) I was relieved, had a cup of tea and went back down for more parts. I was taking a set of back brakes off when I heard my mother say to someone, 'She's up there, between the cars.'

I stood up, expecting to see Clare. Mother was pointing in my direction and was talking to a police officer. I found myself walking over, saying, 'Has the silly little bugger got herself knocked off her bike?' The officer said, 'No, are you Peggy Harris?' 'Yes,' I replied. 'What's wrong?'

All he kept saying was, 'Clare is OK, she is all right.' I found myself saying, 'What's happened? Where is she?' His reply was, 'Someone has attacked Clare but she is all right. She is with police officers at Jurston.'

I couldn't believe what I was hearing. I found myself saying, 'Who's attacked her? Why?' The words were slowly sinking in. The officer wanted me to go with him. 'I'll just get my brother,' I replied. I ran up to Bob's in no time and shouted to him, 'Someone's attacked Clare. I'm going with the police officer to Jurston.' Bob started to bound across the scrapyard asking me who was the attacker down there 'cause I'll kill 'em'! Bob's dog was on his heels, and he had to turn back and shut it in. We both jumped in my car and raced down the lane and caught up with the police officer. He told us to leave the car at the stream that ran across the lane and to follow where he walked, as there were footprints in the sand and dirt. We walked on towards the brook, passing Clare's pushbike leaning against the hedge. We were told to cross over via the stepping-stones.

I'll tell you: it was a long walk up to Jurston. I saw several police cars parked around and a number of policemen stood talking, trying to get phone signals. As I crossed the road to go into a farmyard I saw yet more police cars parked on the bottom green. My mind was starting to race. I was met by an officer, 'Are you Peggy, Clare's mum?' He told me she was all right, just shook up. I wanted to ask her many questions but I was told to just sit with her. Then I heard that they were looking for someone on a moped. I had heard a motorbike go past earlier, but thought it was someone visiting Bob and had carried on taking parts off the car.

Clare threw herself around my neck. She needed that big hug. So did I. Poor Bob sat in shock, feeling useless. I sat Clare on his lap so she could feel safe in his big strong arms. I kept hold of her hand. I could see she had been in a struggle. Her T-shirt had been all screwed up where someone had got hold of her. She showed me the bruises on her legs. I had to know… had he touched her? She said no.

At this point all I knew was that a male with a knife had tried to grab her, there was a struggle and she had broken free and run like the wind up the lane.

It felt like we were sat there for hours. The police had sniffer dogs combing the area to see if the culprit was still about. The owner of the farm arrived outside her gate in her Land Rover, and I could hear her asking calmly, 'What's going on?' She didn't get any answers, and her voice changed as she started to panic. Her husband was in the house and had a long-term illness, and she thought something had happened to him.

A policeman came forward and explained to her what was going on and let her into her yard. She got out of her Land Rover and was calm. She reached us, saying, 'You poor darlings,' offering us tea. She was a breath of fresh air. She told Clare she had horses, and took her over to see them out the back of the farmhouse. Then a helicopter turned up and hovered over us and the horses. You could see the two pilots sitting inside waiting for instructions. We were informed that Clare and I were going to be taken to Newton Abbot police station where they would interview Clare. As it was Sunday they couldn't get hold of a female officer trained to interview children in this situation.

Bob went home across the fields as he wasn't allowed to walk down the lane as it was a crime scene. The police were going to sit at both ends of the lane to ensure no one walked over the footprints, motorbike tracks and struggle scene at the brook, but alas they lost it all as a group of wild ponies walked past the sleeping policemen, right through from Lettaford to Jurston.

We were taken off to Newton Abbot in an armed response car. The two officers were friendly. Clare clung to my hand all the way. We sat in the car at the police station. Our doors were locked and the policemen stood outside. We sat quietly, numb, not knowing what to do, just waiting for the next stage.

Everything was going step by step. We were waiting for a specialist officer, trained in working with children. He eventually arrived, taking us to a property a few streets away. We entered this building and Clare was taken to one side where they took her clothes and DNA and put her in a paper suit which was three times too big for her. We were then put into a room, where three chairs were placed in a triangle. I sat down in front of Clare, noticing that there were cameras in the room. I told her she was to tell the policeman everything she could remember. I told her I would be with her and I wasn't going anywhere.

I was trying hard to be strong for her and to keep calm. Clare looked pale and scared. I kept reassuring her she was going to be all right. She looked at me and confessed that she'd cussed him and called him a bastard as she fought against him. Her innocence pricked my numbness and my eyes filled. 'He is a bastard.' I rolled forward on my knees and gave her a hug.

The policeman entered the room. It turned out the officer had been studying us to see if Clare was a real victim. He was a very friendly officer and put Clare at ease. He asked her a question to see if she could distinguish a lie from truth before starting the interview. She had to start from the very beginning where she first saw her attacker and go through what happened, step by step. When she got to the attack she started talking faster, tears in her eyes, ringing her hands, rustling her paper suit backwards and forwards.

I sat and listened as she explained how a man had jumped out on her, grabbed her and tried to drag her into the bushes, and how he had held a knife to her and threatened to kill her. Her instinct was to fight him off and run away. It seemed surreal as I heard how she fought him off and how she had jumped a five-bar gate in her fear and banged on the door of a local farm. No one was home. She heard the motorbike start up. She jumped back over the gate in panic and raced to the next farm, Lower Jurston, jumped another gate which was even higher, leapt over the flowerbeds and banged on the door. A woman answered the door. She cried out to her that a man had attacked with a knife. The woman pulled her in and bolted the door. This frightened her even more. She was in a stranger's house and the door was locked. The woman phoned the police and handed it to Clare. Panicking Clare paced around and around the kitchen table keeping distance between her and the woman while she waited for the police.

I had to sit, listen, watch and say nothing. She would glance over to me for reassurance. I would squeeze out a smile to let her know she was doing really well.

The police officer took us back to Lettaford by car. They had brought my car up from the brook. By now it was dark and late. The policeman was very good, and talked to Clare about anything and everything. He showed her how the blue lights worked and when it was quiet let her play with them. She thought this was great. I sat in the back of the car and listened as she relaxed. She was safe.

Next morning Clare was up and ready to go to school. She wanted everything to be normal. I was feeling numb, and told her she didn't need to go. I drove her to school and told her where I was to be for the day, if she needed me. I told her I was going in to see her teacher. I spoke to her tutor and he said I needed to go and see the headmistress. He was shocked and very sympathetic. The headmistress was busy, and wanted to know if I had an appointment to see her. I was ruffled by now and found myself saying, 'Well I didn't know my daughter was going to be attacked by a man with a knife yesterday!' 'Oh,' she replied. I told her Clare wanted to be normal and go to school. She wasn't hurt but very frightened. The headmistress asked if the attacker had been caught. 'No, they are still looking for him.'

I never heard from her again; she never showed much interest. I left feeling like I had made a big deal out of nothing. Clare had only had the fright of her life. I was really shook up and upset with the headmistress, and went to see some friends. It was like they didn't believe me; it was like I hadn't said anything important. The way they carried on was as if I was on a normal visit. I am not a tactile person but I needed an arm around my shoulder that day.

The next day the police contacted me. They had picked up someone matching Clare's description. It happened to be a Chagford lad who had turned up the next day and was a little too interested in what was going on. He'd asked, 'Was it all to do with that girl that was attacked yesterday?' He happened to be wearing the same clothes and was on a moped. The police had already taken his brother in for questioning as he had form for a similar crime on the same night it happened.

The next step was to pick him out of a line-up. Every policeman we met was very kind and friendly and put Clare at ease. The duty officer explained to Clare that it was a one-way mirror and that she couldn't be seen. He told her it was really important that she looked at everyone on the line twice.

I knew in seconds she had spotted him. She started to stiffen and started to shake but determinedly looked at each individual twice, just as the policeman had asked her. She walked back to the officer and he asked her if she could tell him the relevant number. Her eyes were filled with tears. 'Three,' she answered. He asked her again, 'Are you sure?' Her voice went into a high pitch. 'Yes,' she replied, spinning round, burying her head into me, shaking and crying. The room fell silent. Everyone in that room felt for her. We had to wait until February for the court case. He was found guilty and was sentenced to four years' imprisonment for his threat to kill. He was out in two years and eight months.

In the meantime my Clare had changed. She was staring at walls, very jumpy, and suffered from anxiety and whiplash. It took her a long time to get over it. She had to have on-going osteopathy treatment, regular trips to the hospital and weekly counselling.

Clare wouldn't talk about what had happened; she couldn't talk about it. She was attacked on Sunday and little Sarah Payne went missing on the Friday after. Clare became transfixed by the case and followed it closely. It was only when they found her body that Clare began to crack. When Sarah was pronounced dead, Clare howled with grief, saying it should have been her instead.

Clare internalised everything and was only a shell of her former self. In my despair I told her to write her thoughts and feelings out on the computer so she could erase it. She just needed to get it out of her head. When I went to bed I would sometimes find letters left from her. They would choke me as I realised how deeply my little girl was hurting.

This is an extract from one of her letters:

Ever since the attack I found it hard to communicate with people close. I sooner shut them off and shut down to a blank. I'm not sure why, partly because I don't want to upset them or to show them how terrified that bastard has made me. For example when I cycle on my way home anyone who moves fast I jump half a mile and pedal as fast as I can. Even now, almost a month later I am jumpy.

To be honest I am petrified. I don't know how to act and I don't want to worry/upset the people around me. I am so angry and hurt that the bastard thought he would do that to me. Whatever he had in his mind he certainly terrified me. He has shaken the solid ground beneath me. I always thought it was the poor other person it happened to. Never to me as I am quite well liked.

I am so angry I can't put it into words. I would like to put him through the feelings I have gone through and hurt that keeps throbbing within me. I was a confident person before this and now I have very little left at the moment.

In the line-up just looking at the slime I was shaking from head to foot. I even cried, I couldn't control myself. They said I had to look at everybody at least twice. As soon as I turned around I saw him sitting there so small and timid.

I wanted to hit myself for being so afraid of a shrimp like that. I could hardly walk knowing he was behind me on the other side of the mirror. The pig that made me so scared and made me into a timid little girl that was so frightened to go to sleep in her own bed she slept with her mum at the age of 13. Even now weeks later I still find it hard to get the words out to talk even to my mum, the closest person to me. When I first met the sod it was his eyes I hated. His eyes were so cold and starey they just stared at me. Every time when I think about what happened I think about those blank blue eyes staring at me. They scare me a lot. I feel like a tiny money spider watching its back. Being squeezed and squeezed almost going to explode but can't get the words out and eat down all the hurt and pain so then eventually turn into a solid ice wall. At the moment no one knows how I feel as I put on the brave, cheery face of the old Clare they know to make them feel better but deep, deep down I am eating myself away. I can't stop this anger and throbbing pain. I don't understand myself. One minute I'm all right then the next minute I am in my world otherwise I am breaking down.

It was heartbreaking to read these letters. I found it very hard watching her staring at the wall, staring into nothing for hours. I didn't know what to do. Nothing I could do would comfort her and make her feel better. When she was small and had hurt herself I would pick her up, hug her, rub her knee, kiss her better, make her laugh, distract her. Now, nothing, nothing I could say or do would make her better. It was going to take time – and it was a long time.

I decided I would get her out the house and so I sent her off to a running club and pushed her into doing lots of sport. Long-distance running, high jump, cross-country competitions… anything to take her mind off it. One of my childhood friends used to take her out riding regularly and let her use one of her horses for the summer, which helped her build up her confidence and made her stronger. Despite it all she pulled herself together and went on to do a university course, find a nice partner and settle down. I am so proud of her as she flew through all her education and got a first-class honours degree.

Looking back I am surprised how naïve and small minded people can be. The rumours at the time were that she must have asked for it, being a 'city girl'. People didn't know who she was, let alone anything about her. At that time she was only 13 and I had purposely kept her young and innocent. People would fall silent when they realised who she was, and would point and whisper. They would give her a wide berth, and that made her feel like an outcast.

Roy with a rabbit and ferret, Cross Park, 2010

MY FRIEND ROY

I met Roy – a short, grey-haired, overweight man with a strong Devonshire accent – in the turkey-plucking shed at Frenchbeer Farm almost 20 years ago. There was a bunch of elderly people in one corner and a lot of younger people scattered around. Roy was talking all the time while he was plucking, talking to Joe and Dez about farming costs and feeds. Joe, who used to be a butcher in Moretonhampstead, told him I was Sammy Harris's daughter.

Over the years he has become a good friend. His soft, foolish nature and Devon tones reminded me of my Father. We have had lots of laughs – mainly at Roy's expense – but I've learnt a lot from him. He taught me how to stone wall, fence, more about repairing vintage tractors and fishing. More often than not Roy would get Dutch courage when he'd had a few and tell me what I meant to him and would often ask me to marry him. Bloody fool!

ROY'S HEART ATTACK

When I first met him Roy told me how he had passed us around Chagford when we were children, when he used to deliver to local farms for Derek Weldon, the feed merchant. He remembered how black we were looking. As the ten days of plucking went on he told me that he had to go on a driving awareness course as he had been in a car accident. The course was in Exeter and he asked if I could show him around Exeter as he hadn't driven there for a while. I agreed.

In the New Year he rang. We drove around Exeter and all the roundabouts we could find. He asked if he could do it all again the following week, just before the course. So we went round and round Exeter again. He said he was stopped on the way home. The cameras had picked him up going round and round Exeter and the policeman wanted to know why. So he explained about the course and how he wanted to practise on the roundabouts as there aren't many in the country lanes.

I thought that would be the last I saw of him. Months went by, and then he rang asking if I wanted a job at the weekend. All I had to do was hammer in the staples as he was hanging stock netting, and could I help him out? That was the start of many days with hours of fencing.

He told me he was having problems at home. His missus was leaving, the house was being repossessed and his main job was coming to an end. He ended up living at an old friend's farm in a caravan in an empty silage pit for the summer. I felt sorry for him, so did his washing and gave him a meal once a week to keep him clean and tidy. He eventually managed to get a job on a grass-drying farm as a rep selling feed again, which came with a house and the use of a barn.

About this time I was looking for a car and didn't have a lot of money. I was offered one for £50, but the body was rusted out. Roy had an idea to get the car anyway – as it had a diesel engine – and to look for a shell. We were lucky; the first paper we looked in there was a Ford Orion being broken for parts. The owner was willing to sell the shell for £15. It was just a shell – no wings, no bonnet, no seats, no suspension – but it didn't matter. I had the rusted-out Ford down at Roy's all complete. It took us many hours and lots of weekends, but bit by bit we made one car out of two from replacing the wire loom and bleeding brakes to welding on wings. Roy sprayed it. I ran this car for seven years.

Roy ploughing at the Silverton Match

The grass farm gave up and Roy was homeless again. He moved just a few miles away to a mobile home on a friend's farm for the next few years. I was still helping him with the fencing, and we had a job out Chagford to put up a fresh fence down a steep field. Roy hadn't been well for the last few days and had a chest infection. He had to dig in the end posts and knock in the rest with the hand banger. We were doing the job for a chap called Tim, and I had to get him to bang in the posts as Roy was in a state and could hardly breathe. I told him he needed to see a doctor. On the Monday he finished the job, Roy visited the doctor who treated him for a chest infection.

Weeks later Roy had been off work for nearly a month. Then he was told he had had pleurisy but would be OK to go back to work the following Monday. He went into work on Friday and told them he would be back on Monday. Roy headed off feeling weary, but as he got closer to home he was in so much pain he had to sit down. Pip his friend turned up. She used to be a nurse and could see he was having a heart attack. When I found out, he was in the RD&E Wonford, Exeter. Eventually I found him in the CCU (Coronary Care Unit). He was very relieved to see me. He had a little cry while telling me what had happened. As he sobbed he told me he needed a triple bypass in the next three weeks and he was on bed rest.

Two weeks later Roy was still in Exeter. The hospital was making arrangements for him to go the Brompton Hospital in London. Time was ticking by. Roy was asked if there anyone to go to London with him, since it was a very big operation. He said he would ask me. I didn't want to go, but I couldn't say no, so made arrangements with work to take a holiday. Roy was taken by ambulance, all blue flashing lights; he said they passed everything. I arrived by bus in the afternoon. Roy was put in quarantine for the first day and then had the all clear. They ran several tests and said he would have his operation the following day. The next morning he said good luck to the fellow from Cornwall he had befriended on the ward, and who had arrived all on his own. He had no one to support him but had learnt from Roy there was accommodation for friends and family, so he arranged for his partner to arrive when he came around. Poor chap looked really frightened when he left the ward. Roy looked scared too, like a rabbit stuck in headlights.

I kept telling him he would be all right, but I didn't know if he would be or not.

Roy was due to have his operation after the chap from Cornwall, around about lunchtime. The doctors had started their ward round, and it wasn't long before they turned up at the foot of his bed. Roy's doctor introduced himself and said, 'Unfortunately due to the lack of intensive care beds we aren't able to do your operation today. We will send you home and see if we can do you next week.' He then turned to the nurse and said Roy could have his breakfast. Poor Roy; he was so upset, but he tried to control his emotions. He started to eat his breakfast, spitting at me, he was so angry: 'I can't go home, I will die. Do they know where I live?' I tried to calm him. I pointed out to the doctor that Roy lived in Devon. A nurse kept saying, 'Don't upset yourself, calm down.' I asked Roy if he was in pain, and he said he had pain in his back. I pointed this out to the nurse. I knew what Roy was thinking. The three weeks were nearly up, he was going to die now – and they wondered why he was upset.

The doctors and nurses rushed around Roy's bed, sticking needles in him, taking blood, putting in blood thinners and pain relief. He was having his second heart attack. They stabilised him after about an hour and an half. He had to remain very calm. He had to have the operation now, but he still had to wait for his breakfast to digest – and his surgeon was still operating on the man from Cornwall.

It was about 3pm when it was time for Roy to go for his operation. I walked along the corridor into the lift down to the next floor. 'You'll be all right Roy.' I squeezed his hand and patted him on the head. He said, 'Will you promise you'll be here when I come round?' I told him again, 'You'll be fine, I'll be here'. The nurse pushed him through the doors of the operating theatre.

I stood there for a moment, thinking 'Will this be the last time I see the poor bugger?' It was a long wait; about five-and-a-half hours. I wasn't able to see Roy until 9am at the earliest the next morning down in the intensive care unit. I waited for an hour as they were washing and dressing him. It was a bigger operation than expected as he had to have five bypasses instead of three. They had taken a vein from the full length of his inside leg, and were very pleased and surprised by how well he was recovering. He was like a little boy when he saw me, delighted and relieved.

By the afternoon he was back on the ward. He had pipes and wires coming from his chest, some attached to bottles, others to monitors. I was allowed to be with him from 9am to 8pm. I had a break from 1 to 2.30pm. The next morning when I arrived he was sitting out. A nurse was helping him to wash as he was very sore. Roy was complaining and saying to the nurse, 'Get off me pipe'. The nurse was an Australian and didn't understand Roy's Devon accent. She turned to me and asked me what he was saying. I said, 'You're stood on his catheter pipe.' She jumped back. 'Why didn't you say?' I said, 'He did, he said get off me pipe!'

We hadn't seen the man from Cornwall for two days, but later that afternoon he appeared. His partner had arrived and was very grateful for the information. She had got the same accommodation as me, so I showed her where to go in and out of the hospital short cuts.

We were in London for five days, then taken home by minibus. The driver didn't hang around. We didn't do much under 90mph, weaving in and out of traffic. We drove so close up behind the back of lorries before overtaking you could count the rivets in the door. I kept thinking, 'Shit! We are going to hit something.' I looked at Roy: he was thinking the same as me. He just wanted to get home.

Then the fun started. I'm not a nurse but I was going to have to help dress him, get him in and out of bed, clean up and get him walking. His goal was to walk two miles in two weeks. The first week was hell for me. I'd put him to bed and he couldn't sleep. They'd said in hospital patients are frightened to go to sleep as they are scared they will not wake up again, and nightmares are common. I would go to bed after sorting him out and sleep lightly, like when I had a baby. Roy would say through the wall. 'Are you asleep?' 'Yes, I was,' I would reply. 'I can't sleep.' I'd ask, 'What to do you want?'

I would sort him out and go back to sleep. I would drop off again and then the voice would come again, 'Are you asleep?' He would do this most of the night. If it wasn't this he was dreaming – saying people were coming through the window, or there was a man under the bed. After a week of this I couldn't be polite any longer. I would ask, 'What's wrong?' If there wasn't anything wrong I would growl, 'Go to sleep.' It was a bit like Chinese torture, and I was knackered. It was worse than having a crying baby.

When I took Roy to the doctor I asked for some sleeping tablets, and drugged him so I could sleep. This helped him get back into a sleep pattern. Roy had started to walk more and more, but then things went into reverse. I had started to go back to work. He was cooking for himself, dressing and washing, so I was going to have a night at home in my own bed. But then one evening Roy called me and said he had been to the doctor with Pip. The doctor had increased his water pills but wanted Roy to go to the hospital. Roy didn't want to go but would I come down? When I arrived he was sat talking to Pip and her husband John, who went home at nearly 11pm. Roy didn't want to go to hospital, and wanted to go to bed, but he was having trouble. He wanted my help to lift his legs and tip him back onto his pillow. He started to shout that his belly was like he was nine months' pregnant. He was filled up with fluid. I was cross with him now. 'It's no good Roy, you need to go to hospital!' He objected. I replied, 'You are going, final!' I went next door to see Pip, and she agreed. We went back down to the mobile home to confront Roy. 'I'll go if you promise to marry me,' he said. I'm sorry to say I was hard. 'You are going to have to die Roy, I am not going to marry you, you are going to hospital!' Then Pip laid into him and told him to not be so silly; he was too old for me and it was more important to get himself sorted.

When he arrived in hospital he had to fight for his life all night long; he could only take five breaths each minute. He was full of fluid and it nearly killed him. At 7am the following day I had a call from a nurse to say he had been very lucky and he would be all right and I could see him at 2pm. It was not long until he was back to work. He was weak for some time, but determined to do everything he had done before.

I spent a week sitting in the Brompton Hospital with Roy while he recovered from his heart operation. I would sit quietly while he slept, watching the nurses going about their jobs. Sometimes you could hear the other patients talking to friends and family members.

One afternoon one old lady was talking about her operation, how she had a pacemaker and she wasn't quite sure what it was for. She was a little confused. She remarked, 'It is just under the skin,' while glancing down at her chest. and then she said she had forgotten to ask the surgeon what kind of batteries it needed.

Two days before his heart attack we had been out to Chagford and bought an old T20 tractor off a neighbour of mine when I lived out

Peggy and Roy repairing a clutch on an old T20 tractor

at the scrapyard. They'd had the tractor parked inside their gate for a few years. I could see it every time I visited Bob. Roy had wanted a T20 for some time; it reminded him of when he was a boy, as his father had bought one for £300. He regretted selling it. We made the deal and paid £100 for a rusty tractor with a seized-up engine and gearbox, but Roy was sure we could get it going.

It was a Tuesday when we picked it up. Roy wasn't well, with a chest infection. We all struggled to load the tractor onto the trailer. It was a job as the brakes were seized on and it had four flat tyres. We eventually arrived back at Roy's place, where we had to back the trailer up the narrow drive. We managed to get the Land Rover and the 17-foot trailer back up near the door of his shed. The next challenge was to get the tractor off and into the shed; it wasn't going to roll off under its own steam. So we had to winch it off, trying to steer it backwards. The steering was hard due to the flat tyres and being a little seized. The back wheel had got too close to the side of the trailer. Roy had shouted at me to steer it, but with him winching it was pulling that way. So I suggested getting a jack under the back axle. I would push against the back wheel with my foot, and Roy was to let it down slowly.

The trailer had a three-inch lip down both sides. I was pushing the bottom of the back wheel with my boot and pushing the top with my hands. The tractor had moved over four inches, just enough. I said, 'Quick – let it down.' Roy turned the handle too quick, letting the tractor drop rapidly, trapping my heel and bending my toes backwards. I couldn't move. The pain was unbearable. I squealed at Roy, 'Jack it up!' He panicked. All he had to do was turn the handle and pump the jack up again. No, not him: he pulled the jack out and shouted at me that I shouldn't have had my foot in the way. I was just shouting, 'Jack it up!' The pain was killing me. I thought I had broken it. He was pissing around. All I kept saying was, 'Put the jack back, turn the handle and pump it up!' No sympathy from Roy. We still had to get the tractor off and into the shed.

Two days later he had the heart attack. I was lucky he didn't have it when I had my foot stuck.

ROY AND THE ROAST PORK

Roy and I were fencing my field one summer weekend. We spent all Saturday banging in posts with a hand hammer when Bob came along, banging like Superman and finishing the rest off in no time. We went back Sunday to hang the wire netting and put up two strands of barbed wire.

Mother called us for dinner. She always cooked Sunday for Bob and decided to cook for me and Roy. We went down the lane to her caravans. She had already dished it up. It was belly pork.

I had given her some frozen belly pork the weekend before. She didn't have a freezer or a fridge and I had suggested she ate it on the following Monday. She hadn't – she'd forgotten – and decided to feed it to us. I asked her if this was the pork I had given her the week before?' 'Yes,' she replied, 'I've washed it in vinegar.' I noticed she was having a fried egg and a slice of bacon instead.

There wasn't much room in the caravan. Bob, Roy and I were sat around a very small table. Mother was stood out by the cooker to eat her meal. Mother's old dog Buster was around our feet, under the table, waiting for scraps. I took one bite of the pork. It was very vinegary and rancid. I looked at Bob; he turned his lip up and curled his nose and started to pass his meat under the table to Buster. There wasn't a word said. I did the same. Poor Roy – he didn't notice and dutifully ate his. Mother nipped out to the next caravan. I said, 'You aren't eating that meat are you?' He replied, 'It doesn't taste very good.' 'Bob and I have fed ours to the dog under the table. This is that pork from last week!'

'Cor, bugger, it be off,' he replied. 'You buggers let me eat it!'

DUCK'S DISEASE

Roy told me a story about when he was young boy in the 1950s, when he lived on a farm at Lake in the parish of Sourton, six miles from Okehampton on the west side of Dartmoor. Roy went to school in Okehampton by bus. He knew a boy called Timothy who was from South Zeal, a few miles on the other side of Okehampton. Roy's granny (his father's mother) lived at South Zeal. She was a very short woman.

One day Roy was playing in school when Timothy told him that his granny wasn't well. He told Roy that she had Duck's Disease. When Roy returned home that evening, he told his father that he had been told that granny wasn't well so his father ordered a taxi and went to see her as they didn't have a car. Roy's father wasn't best pleased when he returned, as there wasn't anything wrong with granny. Next day at school, he asked Timothy, 'What is Duck's Disease?'

Timothy replied, 'Duck's Disease is when your arse is too close to the ground!'

COLLECTING BEAN STICKS

I'd been fishing one Saturday evening with Roy. We got back late so I stayed over. The next morning was bright and dry, but the forecast was for rain. Roy asked me if I would help him collect some bean sticks before the rain set in as his runner beans badly needed sticking.

They were down over the field on the farm he lives on. He wanted 58 straight hazel sticks so we set off in his Suzuki Jeep. My dog Gem sat in the back crammed in among buckets, Roy's fencing tools and general clutter so that the cows wouldn't chase her. She was all right though, as it was only a short trip down across two fields.

The second field was very steep, about 1 in 3. The field was very rough and the jeep started bouncing on the ruts. Gem lost her seating and knocked over one of the buckets beside her. It had some water in it, not a lot but enough to run down the back of my seat and get my bum wet. I turned to see what it was.

At the same time Roy started to turn right, as he was getting ready to park. With the jeep bouncing and Roy turning it to the right, I put my hand out to steady myself, but caught the handle and the door flung open. It all happened in slow motion. Roy stopped, as I flew out. I landed on my back with my head downhill and my legs up in the air, and my feet balanced in the doorway. I lay there

Roy and Peggy fencing at Lower Halstock

for a moment stunned before I looked up at Roy through my boots as I could hear him laughing hysterically. He asked if I was OK between bursts of laughter. 'Even if you're not OK, I'd still laugh,' he told me.

I wasn't too badly hurt, just my pride. I was annoyed at first at him for laughing at me, but then I thought I would have laughed at him if he had fallen out.

MUD IN THE EYE

One weekend Roy and I had 1000 metres of fencing to get up, and it was summertime. Of course, it rained all weekend. We were soaked right through, both days.

We used an old ride-on tractor to pull a trailer to roll out the netting and carry the tools around. It was nearly dinner time and the rain hadn't let up all morning. We rolled the netting out, pulled it up tight and stapled it. We started to head back to the horsebox we used as a shelter. It had a stove in it to heat up food and make tea.

I was driving and Roy jumped onto the trailer for a ride and we headed down the field to the gate. Water had gathered into a big puddle, about six to eight inches deep across the gateway. We were chugging down about 5mph. I turned to go through the gateway when I noticed the front wheel flip out sideways, and without thinking slammed on the brakes. I forgot about Roy on the back. The next thing I saw was Roy flying through the air over my shoulder. He landed headfirst in the puddle and just about emptied it through a 12-foot gateway. He pulled himself up to his knees, spluttering, 'What the hell you be about, stopping like that?'

He was in a hell of a mess – muddy water running out of his eyes and mouth, his head and face just brown streaks. The water went in over the neck of his coat. The state of him! He knelt there wiping the mud out of his eyes. He was giving me a right telling off.

All I could do was laugh and point at the wheel. 'It was the wheel,' I said. I couldn't look at him for the laughing; for a 16-stone man he made a mighty big splash.

RABBITS MAKE ME SNEEZE

Roy asked me if I would like to go shooting rabbits with him at the old farm where he had grown up at Lake. He had permission from the current owner so one Friday evening we parked the car just inside the field gate. As I opened the gate to let Roy drive in I could see that there were loads of rabbits in one field alone. Roy got out his double-barrel 12-bore and filled his pocket with cartridges.

Handing me an old hessian sack we stalked off quietly into the next field. Roy stopped. A rabbit sat just ahead of him, eating. Roy took aim, fired and got it. He beckoned me to come over with the sack to put the rabbit in. It was a full-grown rabbit.

When I was a child I had pet rabbits and they made me sneeze. I thought I must have grown out of it. It wasn't long before Roy fired off again and shot another. He beckoned me to come over to pick up the rabbit, which I stuffed into the sack. Blow me, as I bent down Roy fired off again and got another one. So I rushed over and stuffed that one into the sack. As I walked out into the next field behind Roy I could feel my nose twitching, my eyes started to itch and water. Then all of a sudden out came the three loudest sneezes ever, one after the other. I couldn't stop them.

Roy had just aimed for his fourth rabbit, but with my outburst it took off into the hedge. Roy turned round, scowled and said,

'Shut up! You'll scare the rabbits away!' So we walked down over the field in silence, just the odd sniff from me. I was carrying the sack over my shoulder, the three rabbits weighing heavy. We went into the next field. With the smell of the rabbits in the sack (and probably the smell of the hessian sack too) I couldn't stop sniffing, and out would come another sneeze. I tried to keep it quiet but I just couldn't stop huffing and puffing, sniffing and snorting. This annoyed Roy. The more he told me to be quiet, the worse I got. I told him I couldn't help it, it was the rabbits. So he took the sack and slung it over his shoulder and gave me the gun. My eyes were watering so much I couldn't see the rabbits at the end of the barrel; I could hardly breathe, so we had to give up and go home.

FLASHING LIGHTS

I used to work at a garden at Shillingford Abbot, outside Exeter, once a fortnight for Mr and Mrs Bragg. Mr Bragg had an old Mini Metro. He knew I used to do up old cars and offered it to me. I looked it over; it had four new tyres on, and a new battery. It needed a good clean inside and a new clutch, but for that it was OK. I had nowhere to keep it if I took it, so I asked Roy if I could do it up down his place. He said that it was OK and that he would tow it back for me.

So we arrived at Mr Bragg's one Saturday afternoon late November. The idea was to disconnect the wire of the coil so it didn't overheat and steer the car with the ignition on, so we could use the lights, indicators and wipers as it had started to drizzle. We had to tow the car from Exeter to Bratton Clovelly, the other side of Okehampton.

Roy suggested we went straight down the A30; I didn't want to go that way as I didn't like to be towed over 30mph, so I suggested we took the quiet route through Crediton, Copplestone, Bow, Folly Gate and on to Bratton. We set off about 3pm. I told Roy not to drive too fast but we needed to get on as the light had started to go. We were hooked together with an iron tow bar. With a bang and a bump and jerk we were off.

Roy had an orange flasher on top of the car. The light would catch me in the eyes but I could put up with that, I thought. As the daylight started to go the flashing orange light was making it harder for me to see. As for Roy I think he had forgotten I was there. He was tanking on. I'd glance at the speedo and could see it was registering 50, sometimes 60mph. All I could do was watch his backlights and brake when he did and just hold on tight to the steering wheel. Eventually he pulled in, got out and came to see if I was OK.

I wasn't – and I wasn't pleased. I shouted, 'What's the idea, driving like that?' He replied, 'We gotta get on, it's getting dark.' 'You don't need to drive so fast, I don't like it! I can't see; I feel out of control.' He grinned. 'You'll be all right,' he said, jumping into his car; we were off again.

He started off slowly but it wasn't long before we were back to 50mph. He didn't stop again until we arrived back at his place. He said he daren't stop as he could see I was white with anger. I didn't half give him what for when I got out!

EYES IN THE MIRROR

Roy had been out for the day with a lady friend and her grandchildren on a cycle ride down an old railway track with their black Labrador, Bruno. They had a lovely day. When they got back to his friend's place, Roy unloaded the car and left the boot up, and went in for a cup of tea. It was quite dark when he came out; he put his pushbike back into his car, said cheerio and headed home.

On his way home he heard a noise and thought it was the bike moving in the back, but when he glanced in the mirror he could see a pair of eyes looking at him. This put the wind up Roy and made the hair on the back of his neck stand on end. There was someone in the back of the car… he was trying to think of who it could be, as the seats were down and he had thrown his bike in. Nearly back he heard a noise again, and glanced in the mirror. The eyes were still there. When he got home he jumped out quick and shouted, 'Get out of it!' It moved. It was Bruno the black Labrador. Poor Roy's heart was in his mouth!

EEL

I rang Jack, Roy's brother, to make arrangements to load a skip at the weekend with his digger. Jack told me he'd been out all day cleaning a river; he'd been clearing trees. He was lifting bits of trees out, dumping them onto the bank. He noticed in one bucket-load that there was an eel, so he got out of the digger and gave it a dap over the head three times. He thought he would have it for tea. The farmer came walking down across the field. He didn't notice the eel and stopped right beside it. It started to wriggle and made the farmer jump.

Jack took the eel home in the back bucket of his digger. He said his mother used to cook eel for him when he was a boy, but when he got home he changed his mind about it, so when Roy called in after work Jack gave the eel to Roy. Roy was very pleased to have it as he hadn't eaten an eel for some time.

I put the phone down and it rang again. Now it was it Roy. The first thing he said was, 'Have a guess what I had for tea?' I said, 'An eel! I've just been talking to Jack and he said he gave you an eel.'

Roy started to tell me how he cooked it. He said Jack gave it to him in a bucket. It was about two foot long and it was curled around in the bottom of the bucket and looked like a snake. He tipped it in the sink; he said it was slimy and slippery. Every time he picked it up it slipped out of his hands across the draining board, or into the sink, across the work surface, or onto the floor. Roy said he chopped its head off and it was still wriggling! He couldn't hold it; it was slipping and sliding everywhere. He said he got a piece of string and tied it up to the window latch. I asked, 'What did you do that for?' 'So I could gut it,' he said, 'It just kept wriggling, even after I gutted it and put it in the pan. I had to hold the lid down. The bugger was still wriggling when it was half cooked, the tail was still twitching… It tasted beautiful.'

SMELLY MACKEREL

One May Bank Holiday afternoon I'd agreed to go to a Foot and Mouth farm and help out. It was very hot, and Clare was helping to pull 12½-foot boards off the cowshed walls. Clare got very tired. We were going to stay in Roy's mobile home as he was on holiday. He had asked me to give the cat some mackerel, so I took one out of the freezer and defrosted it in the microwave. I then put two more on a plate to defrost overnight for the next day.

That night I cooked us a meal of lamb chops. Clare loves chops and gravy. We watched television in the front room. Later we made up the beds. I was to sleep on the settee while Clare slept beside me on a Z-bed.

It must have been about an hour and half later that I heard Clare moaning. I thought she had wind and dropped off again, but not for long as the moaning got louder. I asked her, 'What's wrong?' She said she had got a tummy ache. I said, 'Perhaps it's wind – have you been to the toilet today?' 'No,' she replied. 'Well, go see if that will help!' I mumbled grumpily. So she staggered off to the toilet. I must have dropped off again, but soon woke to the sound of faint groaning.

I got up and burst through the toilet door (forgetting that the toilet was right behind it – I almost knocked her head off!). Clare sat slumped over nursing her tummy, still groaning. 'Haven't you been yet?' I said abruptly.

I took one look at her in the light and could see there was something really wrong. She was a strange colour and felt clammy. I started to question her about where the pain was. It was on her lower right-hand side. I felt it might be appendicitis but I wasn't sure what side it was so I decided to ring a friend. It was gone 12.30am and I was miles from any help. She agreed with me that the appendix is on the right side and told me to call a locum doctor. I told her I had no number, so she found the number and rang me back. I rang the number and they asked what number I was calling from. I didn't know that either. I asked them to do 1471 but that was impossible; and the operator needed the number so that the doctor could call me back.

I was stuck. I could have called an ambulance but I knew it would take a long time (and that Clare might only have had wind). So I rang Wendy back, and she'd done 1471 so could give me my number! I called the locum line again, but it still wasn't going to work; I knew the address but I couldn't explain how to get there. Too many lanes to turn down and I didn't know the names of the crossroads. So I told the doctor it would be quicker for me to bring Clare to Okehampton Hospital.

I bundled Clare into the car and set off to Okehampton. On the way she asked me if it was serious. I didn't know what to say so, I told her to wait and see what the doctor had to say, as it may be just wind. We fled down the A30 and turned off the slip road for Okehampton. I was speeding at this point and didn't see the T-junction; it came up a bit quick. I had to brake rather hard; luckily it was the middle of the night as there was no one around. At this point Clare asked me to slow down as she realised I had started to panic.

I arrived at the hospital and the doctor examined her and said my suspicions were right and he would call for an ambulance. He said, 'She may go to Plymouth or to Exeter.' I would have to wait. I told the doctor that we lived in Exeter and it would be quicker for me to take her. The doctor rang Exeter and told them we were on our way.

I was quite worried by now and had to prepare Clare that she might need an operation. She said, 'I don't care, just get rid of the pain.' It was nearly 2am and there wasn't anyone around. It was a very still night as we sped up the main road, breaking the speed limit. I said to Clare, 'I just hope we don't get stopped.' But if we had I think the police would have given us a police escort.

At Exeter the nurse was expecting us, and showed us into a cubicle. 'The doctor will be along in two ticks,' she chirped. I was sat by Clare who lay on the bed. We whispered to each other while listening to the noises of rushing footsteps and the moaning and groaning of other patients.

After a while the doctor arrived. He was a short man; he couldn't have been any more than four feet tall. He looked like a little boy. Clare's eyes rolled over to me as much to say, 'Is that the doctor?' He went to examine her but couldn't reach, even after lowering the bed. He said, 'Be back in a moment' and reappeared holding a box. After examining her he agreed it was it was appendicitis and she would need an operation. Time had ticked on and he gave Clare pain relief after finding her a bed on a ward. She had X-rays and blood tests; by now it was 5.30am and she was asleep. They decided that they would let her sleep and operate later.

Later in the morning, when the operation was over, I was feeling like crap. The lack of sleep and the trauma had taken its toll. I found it all very upsetting and frightening until she was awake again.

Then I remembered the mackerel. I had only left a note for the farmer saying I had gone to the hospital; I didn't even think about the mackerel. I tried several times a day to phone the farmer but couldn't get through. I knew Roy wouldn't be back for a week and the fish would be stinking by then, but I didn't want to leave Clare and go all that way to sort it out as it's nearly 50 miles away.

I hadn't got hold of the farmer all week. When Roy arrived home the farmer told him I had left a note saying I had gone to the hospital and he had not seen or heard from me since.

Roy opened the door to his mobile home and was met with the stink of death. He could see our beds and bedding through the half-open door to the sitting room. He rushed closer, panicking, as he thought we had gassed ourselves to death. He stood in the doorway looking down at the scattered bedding. When he realised that there were no dead bodies he slowly turned round to see where the smell was coming from. On the corner of the kitchen unit he found the stinking mackerel, crawling with maggots. They were everywhere, on the floor and all over the unit. He realised that something was up as we had left in such a hurry.

I was worried he would be cross to come home to such a stink but he wasn't; he was really glad that it was only dead fish.

OLD DUCKS AND OLD GEESE

I was out at Great Ley one day and a neighbour asked if we could take in some ducks and geese. As Margaret already had geese and chickens she felt they would fit in. When they arrived some looked old. It turned out they belonged to her daughter, who couldn't keep them any more as she was expecting a baby.

The next day Roy turned up. He had come to help kill his chickens that we were raising for him. I said to him 'Do you want a goose and a couple of ducks?' His eyes lit up. 'Cor, yeah.' Roy likes duck and goose. I showed him the ones we were keeping. He rejected one duck, saying it was as old as the hills, so he had a goose and just a couple of ducks. He killed them and plucked them and put them in his car.

A minute later Margaret's neighbour came by, out walking her dog. She asked me if the ducks and geese had settled in. I said that they had, and then she said 'You won't eat them, will you?' She had never mentioned this before! I put Roy on the spot by saying, 'Roy's having some, aren't you?' Roy spluttered and replied, 'Yeah, I'm going to give them a good home!' As she walked off he turned to me and said, 'You shit, the only home I've got is a cold white one. Yeah, I'll give 'em a good home!'

The next time I saw Roy he wasn't happy. 'That goose was as tough as old Nick. I nearly broke me teeth!'

ROY BLOWS UP THE STOVE

Clare and I were visiting Roy down in Bratton Clovelly. He was lighting the Rayburn to cook us dinner. Clare and I were out on the lawn playing with the cat.

Roy kept going in and out of his bungalow, chopping lighting sticks and fetching coal. He was disgruntled, as he couldn't light the fire. Later he went into the garage and came out carrying a little tin in his hand. 'Won't be long now,' he called, as he disappeared indoors again. It wasn't long before I heard the Rayburn roaring up the chimney. I looked up and saw a lot of smoke. All of a sudden there was a loud bang and a great puff of black smoke exploded out of the chimney, followed by shooting flames. We rushed up to the window and peered in. The room was full of smoke and Roy was kneeling on the floor in front of the Rayburn, his face black with soot. As I saw he was all right I couldn't stop myself laughing. I went in and the whole kitchen was covered in a thick layer of black soot. I had to clean his eyes out before we could clear up. I just couldn't stop laughing at him. He looked as if he had used his head to clean the chimney.

I asked him what he had done to the Rayburn, and he said, 'It wouldn't light.' 'Well you got it going now! What did you light it with, a bomb?' I asked. 'No, a drop of diesel,' he replied grumpily. 'I'd been trying to light it but it wouldn't pick up, so I put a drop of diesel in to help it along but by the time I'd fumbled with the match it'd turned to gas and exploded.' He paused for a moment as he felt his singed eyebrows. 'The flames came out and wrapped around my ears, it nearly deafened me.'

'You silly bugger,' I chuckled. 'You could have blown your head off and you've cracked the chimney pot.'

I spent the rest of the afternoon cleaning the kitchen up for him. The soot had even got into the cupboards and the ceiling was plastered. I was none too pleased. After a bit Roy said, 'Well, I won't have to sweep the chimney for a bit.' I was not amused.

ROY AND I WENT RABBITING

It was late November in 2010 and it had snowed. Roy and I had decided to go ferreting one Sunday afternoon as the snow was still lying. I said it would be a good idea because we would be able to see where the rabbits had gone into the hedge and which holes we needed to net.

On the farm where Roy lives there are lots of rabbits in the hedges. We netted up several holes that had rabbit tracks leading down the burrows. We then walked down the field and through the gate to net the exit holes on the other side of the hedge. It was the lower side which was sheltered from the wind and not so cold. So I told Roy to stay this side (he takes warfarin and feels the cold badly).

Once we had covered all the holes I went back to get the ferrets out of the box. We only have two: 'Biter', a polecat ferret, and 'Fatso'.

Roy with his ferret in the snow, 2010

Fatso is a Silvermit ferret, mostly white with a ratty looking face. He's twice the size of any normal ferret. They both stink like sweaty socks.

Getting them quickly out of the box I put them in different holes, making sure I didn't get bitten, then waited. It wasn't long until Roy shouted, 'Aye up!' 'What?' I said. 'Got a rabbit.' he replied. Then he shouted again, 'There's another!' I shouted over the hedge, 'Grab it then!' I heard Roy shout in pain. 'You'll have to come and help me!' 'Why?' I replied, 'I'm watching this side!' 'I got a rabbit in a net in each hand and I got a bloody ferret hanging off my finger! You've got to help – come on!' he shouted.

'I'm coming,' I replied, running down the field, through the gate and back up the other side. As I puffed closer I could see Roy with a rabbit in a net, still alive, held between his knees. The other rabbit, held by its back legs, was still kicking in the net and Roy was holding Fatso up, to take the weight off his finger. His teeth were latched in with Roy's blood around his whiskers and dripping on the floor. That ferret wasn't letting go anytime soon. I could see blood pouring from Roy's finger. 'What do you want me to do?' I asked. 'Pinch his toe.' 'That's cruel!' I replied. 'No crueller than what the bugger's doing to me!'

Peggy and Sam

THE WOMAN I CALLED MOTHER

There are reasons why Mother treated us like she did over the years; it wasn't easy for any of us. But relationships change over time – circumstances too – and the last piece in this book brings the story of our relationship right up to date. She was a very hard woman and didn't show much love (and if she did I must have been looking the other way). When we were young and living at the scrapyard she would punish us three kids very hard. She would bang our heads together and whack us around the ear with her bare hands when we passed her on our way to bed. It didn't matter if you hadn't done anything: we all got the same.

MOTHER'S LIFE AT THE SCRAPYARD

Over the years, Mother lost her feminine side. She worked hard and dressed practical. She used to dress in jeans, welly boots and a flat cap, and wore a leather jerkin.

Father would stress her out. He would keep on at her and make fun of her. She worked hard all day, fetching and delivering scrap, had to make dinner when she got home and do the washing. We never had running water or electric. We all had to fetch drinking water from the river a quarter mile down the lane. The toilet was a large bucket and Mother had to empty it each week; she would dig it into the garden. I was glad I never had to do it.

I remember her accusing a customer (who used to come regular to buy antiques) of crawling under the caravan in the late evening to listen to her and Father's conversation (of course this wasn't true). She was always accusing me of something; I had taken something that was missing. The accusations would go on for weeks, months, and come up years later.

One time Jim had a girlfriend, who'd visit at weekends. It wasn't long before Mother started accusing her of pinching her knickers. I told her not to be so silly; she wouldn't want her knickers. Then it was her shoes. I told her they wouldn't fit, and so it was back to the knickers again. Mother decided to buy men's Y-fronts. She said she had sewed up the Ys and was wearing them back to front. Her comment was, 'Let her pinch them!

125

Mother was a person you just kept out of the way of and said very little to. I don't really know my mother; she's like a closed book. When she does talk about things, it's a load of rambling rubbish. She talks about guardian angels, and how her dead grandfather is helping her through life; or how someone's marking her, or the neighbours or people are spying on her. She won't listen to reason. Her ranting and accusing has just pushed her sons away; they don't want anything more to do with her.

WHEN MOTHER LEFT

At the end of June 1986 she left, without warning. I knew she hadn't been happy for years. I was pregnant and I didn't know how to tell her. I felt she would have made me get rid of it, or fed me something that would have ended it, as she was well into her herbs.

It was a Friday morning. Mother and I had taken a load of metals to Exeter, and I was driving. When we had delivered the scrap she told me she was leaving and wasn't coming back. I asked her where she was going. She said her guardian angel had told her that she had to go to Dorset. I had to drop her at Exeter service station, from where she hitchhiked and walked to Dorchester. It took her two days. There she found a job as a housekeeper, for an old man. It was a month before she made contact. She wrote to Bob, and in the letter was a phone number. When Father was out I would give her a ring to make sure she was all right. She seemed to be happy.

Christmas was coming and I hadn't told her I'd had my baby but an aunt, her sister, was going to write and give her the news. So it was strongly suggested that I told her myself. She took it well, but it wasn't long before she was writing me letters on how to get rid of a baby, hot baths and going for a run after sex, keep your hand over your ha'penny and crap like that. This went on for weeks. In the end I said if I was going to have any more babies it would be my choice. Not long after that she was writing and saying the old man she was working for was going through her letters and that he wanted her. So she invented her own unique alphabet. Nobody can read what she writes now, it's all in code.

I went to see her with my aunt one time. I told her I would pick her up if she wasn't happy, and in the end she was there for just over a year before she asked me to fetch her. I fetched her in an estate car and it was full to bursting with her things. When she'd left home she went in what she was stood up in. I know I sent two suitcases up with a lorry driver.

Mother has a stroke

When Mother came back to Devon she stayed in Chagford with her mother and sisters. Her sister Angel helped her find a short-let accommodation before moving to a one-room bedsit in Moretonhampstead. I went to see her one Wednesday afternoon. She was sat in her chair and I was having a cup of tea. She was going to walk the dog, and was waiting for me to go, when she said, 'Oh, my head.' She told me that she had a sharp pain and could see two of me. I said, 'Don't worry, I'll take the dog.' So I took the dog for a quick walk, thinking if she wasn't any better when I returned I would take her to the hospital. When I got back I couldn't get in, and she took ages to open the door. I could see she was ill; she was pale and all weak down one side. I pushed the dog inside then helped her across the road into my Mini and drove her up to the hospital. I half carried her in, and they asked if she normally looked like this. I replied, 'She looks like death warmed up.'

They told me she'd had a stroke, but that there weren't any beds and to bring her back in a couple of days. They asked if she could stay with someone. I knew she couldn't stay with me; there was no room. I went to see her sister Myrtle who lived just down the road, and explained what had happened. Myrtle told me to bring her down. When we arrived, she had made a fish dinner and placed it on Mother's lap. I could see Mother was ill; she just sat, staring at her plate. It was a year before she was fit again.

Back at the bedsit she started saying there was someone climbing the drainpipe. We all just thought 'Mother's at it again.' She even reported it to the local policeman, who asked my brother Bob one day about Mother's state of mind. His reply was, 'She's as nutty as squirrel shit, take no notice.' But there was someone coming down the drainpipe; she was right. She took the law into her own hands and she greased the drainpipe. There was a young girl upstairs who had a visiting boyfriend. The rule was no overnight visitors, and the front door was locked at all times. The easy way out was down the drainpipe. Mother cured him; it nearly broke his neck!

Then she moved to a bigger flat. She said she had visitors when she was out so she changed the locks. Then it was ghosts. I had moved away to Exeter; my life was upside down. It was a while before I saw her.

MOTHER MOVES BACK TO LETTAFORD

In the middle of it all, my father died. Nine months later Mother moved back to the scrapyard with Jim and Bob, and lived in a caravan at the bottom of the yard. She made herself a garden, as she was keen on gardening. Jim was living with a girlfriend; Mother started accusing him of stealing things, like a chipped cup and a rack out of her cooker. Jim moved away. I used to visit her and so she started on me. She had lost her secateurs and as I was working in gardens, she said I must have stolen them. It wasn't long after my birthday. She had given me a card with a tenner in it, so I gave the money back to her and said, 'You'd better buy yourself a new pair as I haven't had them.' But in her eyes this meant I was guilty.

One Sunday Clare went down to see her. She told Clare she was a fly in the eye, and didn't want to know her; I just saw red. I knew Mother was just being nasty; Clare was only six. I had a go at her and I couldn't talk to her for 12 months.

She had it in for her neighbours; she accused them of being able to talk to animals. She said they had sent various animals – a sheep, ponies, and a squirrel – up to the garden to eat the vegetables. All these animals roam free on the commons and in woods around the moor. She confronted the ponies; she looked them straight in the eye and told them she knew. She screamed at the squirrel like a banshee; she told the sheep they were too thick and ran over everything. Mother had read a book about talking to animals. She had told a visitor about this book, and she believed this person had passed on the information to the neighbours; they had then bought the book and sent the animals into her garden.

After this she accused them of marking her, and I asked her what she meant. She took me out in the lane: 'See, there.' It was a white splat. I looked closer; it was bird shit. It looked to me that a bird had been on its nest all night and had dropped its load as it flew out. Not to Mother; it was the neighbours who were leaving white marks and stones out in the lane (a rough track). If she saw that a stone had moved, the neighbours had moved it just to get at her.

You get a lot of atmospherics on the edge of the moor, giving you a bad picture on the TV. Mother told me Father was sat on the aerial fiddling with the picture. Another day she told me Father was making her pee down her leg, I told her not to be so silly and to bear down a bit harder. He had been dead for ten years.

MOTHER LOSES HER MONEY

Mother had sent off for a pair of pinhole glasses she'd found an advert for in a magazine; they were £40 a pair. She sent off for them abroad but it was a fraudulent set-up. They changed her £40 into £4000, duplicated the cheque and emptied her bank account of £8000. The bank contacted her as she was overdrawn. She showed me the letter and I decided to take her to the police station. She told the policeman she felt it was the neighbours. I couldn't believe it. I tried to explain to her what had happened but she wouldn't have it; in her eyes it was the neighbours. Luckily the bank refunded her. They wanted her to be a witness, but after meeting her she heard no more.

'PREFER DRILLER'

Mother had decided that she was going to get a company in to drill a borehole for water. She never discussed with Bob where she was going to have the hole drilled. Bob came home and found a man drilling in the middle of his field, just where he didn't want it. There was a heated discussion and the drilling was abandoned. But Mother had taken a fancy to the man who was operating the drill. I never saw him so I don't know what he looked like. Mother was talking about leaving again and was going to put an advert in the paper for a live-in housekeeper job. She was about 75 at the time. My friend Hazel asked me, 'Have you seen your mother's advert in the newsagent?' 'No?' I replied, 'I know she was going to apply for a live-in housekeeper job.' Hazel said, 'I didn't understand the advert, what's the driller bit?'

The advert read: 'Looking for housekeeper live-in job. Cook, clean, look after children, prefer driller.' I said to Hazel, 'She won't get a reply. She can't cook, she wasn't a good mother, she wouldn't look after modern-day kids and she fancies the man who came to drill the borehole.' This just made Hazel laugh.

MOTHER GOES TO HOSPITAL

In May 2002 Mother hurt her back. I suggested she went to the doctor but she wouldn't. She did see an osteopath but it didn't help; she'd taken a dislike to him. She had upset Bob, and he didn't want anything to do with her. A lady up the road took Mother shopping for a while, until she took a dislike to her too. So I was going from Exeter once a week to take her shopping. It was a proper chore.

One Wednesday night I could see she was in pain; she was bent right over, head down by her knees, and taking aspirin for pain relief. She said she couldn't go shopping, and gave me a list. I said she needed to see a doctor, and she told me Bob had taken her a few days earlier and she was to go back on the Friday. I did her shopping, and went to see Angel. I told her I felt Mother needed to see a doctor but knew she wouldn't go with me. So I asked Angel to persuade Mother that she needed to go to hospital.

It worked; we took her to hospital. When the nurse undressed her I couldn't get over how white she was. I found myself saying, 'Cor Mother, you're white!' The nurse said she was very anaemic. They found she had a bleeding ulcer and only four pints of blood left in her body. They operated on her and she spent several weeks in hospital.

I decided that she couldn't go home to a leaking caravan. Bob wasn't talking to her; it wasn't safe for her to go back there. I asked the hospital doctors to assess her as I felt she was suffering from paranoia, but Mother was on her best behaviour and they felt she was all right. I told Mother that she couldn't go back home, and she agreed that she wasn't happy there any more. I told her that if she didn't accuse my neighbours or my friends of anything she could come and stay with me and I would help her to get rehoused once she was well enough. She stayed with me for five months, still on her best behaviour. No bogeymen. I joked that it must have been down to the new blood they'd given her!

MOTHER GETS REHOUSED

While Mother was staying with me my osteopath helped her to stand up straighter, to enable her to look after herself. She managed to get rehoused in an almshouse. I fetched her belongings from the caravans and got her some new things. She was really pleased with her new flat, and I was happy for her.

One day I found she'd put a chain and padlock on the front door, and I thought it had all started up again. She'd decided the woman upstairs was coming down when she was out and pinching her knickers. She told me the woman upstairs had been a spy in the war, so she knew how to get into places. I told Mother not to be so silly; the woman was in her late eighties. I found out this poor old lady was very ill; she had heart trouble, was a little deaf and was fighting cancer. She had trouble walking, let alone breaking in. My mother met her in the local shop and remarked harshly, 'I know you've been in and had my knickers!' then walked away. I told Mother off.

Next time the old lady saw Mother and asked her what she'd meant, Mother snapped and told her to stop raking up the dirt. The poor old lady was bewildered. Mother had it in for her for some time. It didn't matter what I said; she was convinced she was spying on her, so she took on a private investigator. When he heard that she was accusing an 87-year-old woman, he didn't want the case. He rang me to see if I knew what she was doing, and I told him to go along with her and prove that there wasn't anyone going into her flat. He said she'd soon find someone else to pick on and that he felt she had senile dementia. I said, 'Don't worry, she's been like it all my life.' He rang back a few days later saying that she had cancelled his services and had solved the problem by putting talcum powder around the flat.

One day I went to see her and the chain and padlock had gone. I said, 'You're happy.' 'Yes!' she replied. 'She's dead!' She was jumping up and down with joy, clapping her hands. I was disgusted. I told her she was in the wrong and was being disrespectful to the dead. I told her, 'She was a very sick old lady.' I just hope that she didn't ever know what Mother was thinking.

After a few weeks a new person moved in. She had a male friend who came and spent everyday with her. Mother started on them, accusing them of spying on her again, as they spent a lot of time looking out of the window.

I used to go and see her once a week, most weeks. She wasn't bothered whether I was there or not. She never asked me how I was or what I'd been doing.

MOTHER TURNS ON ME

When my friend Roy had a heart attack I went to London for his operation, then stayed with him for a week when he got home. So I hadn't seen Mother for two weeks or more, and thought she'd be glad to see me as she knew I'd been helping Roy. I called round, and she sat down and just put her nose in the television. She didn't want to talk; she didn't offer me a cup of tea, like usual. I wasn't really bothered but I felt it was rude to ignore me; she was only watching rubbish on the TV. So I got up and said, 'If you don't want me just say so, because I can go.' Her reply was, 'Oh come again.' So I walked out. She came out behind me to get her parking permit back. I told her I felt she was being rude; after all, I'd made the effort to come and see her. She showed no emotion and just said, 'Come again.' I stomped off, saying, 'What's the point?' (I was pissed off).

I didn't go again for nearly three weeks. One Thursday morning I knocked on the door. She said, 'Who is it?' (which she always does). I replied, 'It's me', as she usually recognises my voice. 'Who?' 'Peggy,' I replied. 'Oh, you.' I wondered what the matter was. She opened the door, 'You ain't coming in here!' 'What's wrong?' I asked. She replied 'It's you, it's bin you all the time!' 'What you talking about?' 'It's bin you all the time, I've bin blaming them, upstairs and it's bin you, you bin pinching every time you come here! I can't turn my back on you.' I couldn't believe it. I said, 'What have I pinched?' 'You know!' 'I don't!' I said, 'I haven't pinched a thing.' She said 'I've never liked you, you're just like your father, I didn't like him!' 'Well, what am I supposed to have pinched?' She said, 'My book, *Talking to Animals*, a pot of ointment, a flannel.' She wasn't upset; she was cold and very much in control. She shut the door on me.

I went back to the car feeling very upset and rejected. When I got home I rang her, but she was just the same. She said I had pinched a silver spitfire brooch and had given it away when I was young, and I was always pinching things to give away to people. She had turned on me again. The only way she would believe me was for me to own up and say I was to change, as she didn't like me for who I was. I told her she would have a long wait as I wasn't going to own up to something I hadn't done, and I was what she had made me and she should be glad how I turned out and it was no thanks to her. She just said again, 'I've never liked you!' and slammed the phone down.

MOTHER TURNS ON CLARE

One time Clare was going to visit my mother. I warned her that Mother was being funny and that she didn't want to see me any more. I told Clare to be careful, as she was likely to pick on her. After hearing what Mother had said to me Clare waited three weeks before she plucked up the courage to give her a ring. She made arrangements to meet on the following Thursday.

That evening I received a phone from Clare saying, 'Have a guess what Gran said to me? You won't believe what she said!' Then she went on to tell me how the conversation had gone. On the whole it went quite well; they'd nattered about different jobs Mother had done in her life, comparing them to what Clare was doing in hers. Clare said that Mother had been reminiscing about the past, then she paused and went quiet. Clare asked if she was OK. Mother had forgotten what she was talking about, so Clare reminded her. This was when Mother's tone and conversation changed.

Out of nowhere she started to accuse Clare of abusing her cat when she was about five years old. Clare was taken by surprise and asked Mother what she meant. Mother told Clare that she had put itching powder up her cat's arse, and had been into Moreton and had done the same to her mother's friend's cat because she could smell it. Clare was gobsmacked. She couldn't believe her ears as Mother ranted on. She accused Clare of sitting quiet and having a very straight face and not saying anything. Clare explained to Mother that she couldn't believe that she would accuse her of such a thing, then pointed out that she didn't see her when she was five as we didn't have any transport. When she'd pointed out the flaws in Gran's accusations, she started to back down and accuse someone else. Her mood changed again and she invited Clare back to dinner the following week. Clare did go, expecting another bombshell, but Gran was all right that time. Clare decided to wait a few months before venturing back.

Eventually she turned on Clare and said she was too much like her own mother and she didn't want to see her any more.

Peggy with a barrow load of rabbits at Throwleigh

THE LATER YEARS

Time moves on, and despite everything that's happened Clare and I are doing fine. Clare has graduated from university with a first-class honours degree in fine art and is now living independently upcountry. She is the lady that I had hoped she would grow up to be. For my part I've been working at Newberys scrap merchants for nearly ten years now.

NEWBERYS

I started to work for G H Newbery & Son in Exeter at the end of January 2005 after being made redundant from Spangles Car Wash, which had gone bankrupt. I knew Russell, one of the family owners, from back in the days when we delivered scrap from Lettaford, and I would often chat to him when I was picking up cars for cleaning from the Vauxhall car dealers. He kept on offering me a job but I didn't want to go back into scrap. I knew it wouldn't be the same as working from home: if you wanted a rest you could just sit down, and if you wanted a cup of tea you could go and make one. Working for someone else, you would be on their time; breaks would be fixed and you would be worked hard until it was time to go home.

I had a number of interviews to do with car valeting but nothing had come of them. In December I did turkey plucking up on Dartmoor to tide me over, but now that it was January I was picking up my own scrap metals from my shed to sell as a last resort before having to sign on the dole. On delivering the metals to Newberys I asked Russell if a job was still going. His mother was in that day and she gave me an interview. They had a discussion when I left, and not long after I got home she rang me and offered me a job for three days a week. I've been at Newberys ten years this coming January!

Newberys is very much like our scrapyard used to be, and certain customers you have to watch. A few can be light-fingered. On one occasion I'd just served a customer who had brought in a load of copper tanks. I was on my own and hadn't had time to get them down to the baler before the next van backed into the warehouse. Two passengers jumped out and crowded around me, saying, 'Hello darling, how are you?' The driver had gone to the back of the van and opened the door. These two were blocking me and I knew they were ones to watch and would probably try to pinch the copper tanks. I pushed past and the driver was making out he had just taken a tank out of his van. I told him that that the tank wasn't his as I had just weighed it, along with the others, from the last customer. All three swore black's white on their mother's life that it was theirs. I told him that it was funny then that I was one short. I knew bloody well it wasn't theirs; I can count, so I went to get someone out of the office to back me up. Fortunately they didn't get away with it.

Some people would take the scrap iron and throw it out on the iron pile. If they see a bit of copper, or something of value, they will pick it up if no one is looking and then bring it into the warehouse for weighing. There was a lad who did this a couple of times and one occasion I walked around the vehicles unloading and a customer had thrown out an old lawn mower engine. I had spotted it on the ground and this lad came into the warehouse and pulled this engine out his van. He wanted to sell it as irony ally (dirty aluminium) as it is worth more than steel. I said to him 'That's not yours!' He swore it was, so I told him I had seen it come in from another customer but he wasn't having it, and swore it was his. Once again I had to get someone from the office. But it wasn't long before he tried it on again, this time with a piece of copper pipe. He swore it was his so I said 'If it's yours, go into the office and tell them! He soon wound his neck in.

BLACKBIRD

Our family scrapyard ran for 45 years with not much of a problem. Then all of a sudden it changed overnight – rules, regulations and business tax flying in. To comply with it all my brother Bob had to apply to the National Park for planning. They weren't helpful; they didn't want a scrapyard on Dartmoor.

The Environment Agency said there had to be a smaller compound and drainage tanks for waste oil and acid. The scrap prices had dropped to rock bottom and it wasn't worth the struggle, so Bob closed down. The Environment Agency said the land was contaminated – but you tell the wildlife that.

I visited Bob one evening and I could hear this funny noise. I said to Bob, 'What's that noise?' It sounded like an engine was rumbling in the distance. We walked up to the hedge where the noise was coming from and there we could see hundreds of frogs hopping and croaking. I mean there were hundreds of them and this place was supposed to be condemned: but no one had told the frogs.

Even when there were hundreds of cars the wildlife moved in. The birds were always nesting under the bonnets, in the headlight hole, backlight hole, in the boot. The fieldmice made nests under the bonnets. Squirrels were always hiding their nuts in the cars.

One day when I went up to see Bob he needed to use his old Hymac, a swing shovel. It had been parked up for some time as the yard had been shut down. We needed it now to move something very heavy. We went to put some fuel in it and as we went to lift the bonnet a blackbird flew out and nearly knocked me off the step. She had made a nest beside the engine; there were three green eggs. I told Bob that he shouldn't be long using the machine as the bird needed to get back to her eggs. 'All right,' he said. I left him to get on with what he was going to move as I had to go to Moretonhampstead to pick up Clare, who'd been horse riding.

When we returned I noticed Bob hadn't put the machine back where it had been parked for all that time. When I walked up to his place and passed the spot where the Hymac had been parked I could see the blackbird flying about looking for the nest; she was trying every possible flight path. She would land on the ground roughly where the nest would have been and you could see she was thinking, 'It was here!' Then she would try again from a different direction and land in the same spot and look about, and you could see she was thinking the same thing.

I found Bob and said, 'That bird's looking for her nest.' He said, 'Can't it go down to where I parked it and find it?' 'No,' I said. 'She can only find it in her flight path so put the Hymac back.'

He did and we left the bird to find her nest. About four months later when I was up at Bob's I went to the Hymac and noticed that the blackbird had hatched her three eggs and reared them.

FERRET DOWN A HOLE

I had caught up with Chris Chapman around Christmas. He showed me a picture of him and his ferret when he was a young man. He said he used to love going rabbiting, and he was thinking about getting a ferret for his son Jed. I told him my daughter had two ferrets that were quiet and less likely to bite, so good for Jed to handle for the first time. Chris was very enthusiastic; he said that he still had his rabbiting nets. I told him I didn't think Clare would want her ferrets going down a rabbit hole as they were townie ferrets; they lived indoors with the central heating on, and she would be afraid to lose them.

Chris Chapman with Peggy at Cross Park, Throwleigh

We made arrangements to meet on New Year's Eve in the afternoon. Clare introduced her two ferrets to Jed; he was a little nervous to start with, keeping his thick gloves on. Chris was so keen to get on he produced his rabbiting nets. I told him Clare was worried she would lose them. Chris told me he had never known a ferret not to come back out of a rabbit hole and there were plenty of rabbits in his fields, so I persuaded Clare to let him try Benson, as he'd been used for rabbiting with his previous owner.

It was a very cold afternoon. The ground was frozen hard as we walked down over the field: Chris with his nets slung over his shoulder, Clare with her ferret stuffed in her coat with his head popped out over her collar, and Jed with an air rifle. I was hoping it wasn't going to take long as I was feeling the cold.

We helped to put the nets up over the rabbit holes on one side of the hedge. Chris and I then walked down the field, over the gate and back up the other side. Clare and Jed stayed on the netted side, talking. We laid a few more nets on our side of the hedge. When we were ready Clare handed Benson over the hedge to Chris who put him in a hole. It wasn't long until he came out the other side, where

Clare posted him back down a different hole. After we had worked him to and fro down a couple of the holes there was still no a sign of a rabbit, so Chris decided to put him down a hole a few metres away from the hedge. You could see that there were lots of rabbits around from the droppings on the ground. Chris put Benson at the entrance of the burrow and he disappeared down it. I thought to myself: he won't be long, he'll soon find a rabbit in there.

Five minutes passed and Clare shouted over the hedge, 'Have you seen him yet?' 'Not yet, but he's OK.' There was still no sign of him after half an hour. Clare and Jed were still nattering away together. I was starting to get worried. Chris couldn't believe it. He quietly told me, 'I'll buy her another ferret.' I told him, 'Clare won't want another ferret, she wants Benson!' Chris whispered to me, 'I'll stay here all night until he comes out!'

By now Clare was getting pretty anxious and came over to our side of the hedge with Jed to see if she could call Benson out. We had a squeaky toy on a string and Jed had some high-pitched ring tones on his phone and we all tried calling down the hole, 'Benson, what's this?' as that's what Clare usually called to get him to come. It was so cold Clare was afraid he had gone to sleep, which was particularly worrying as ferrets can sleep for up to 22 hours a day.

Chris then had the idea of fetching some drain rods, so while he was gone I continued to call Benson on my hands and knees with my face down the rabbit hole, feeling a fool and wondering what the neighbouring farmers were going to think as my voice echoed in the cold still air.

Chris arrived back with the drain rods; Clare was worried we were going to put them down the same hole as Benson. Chris reassured her he was going to put the rods down the next rabbit hole, a little way from where he went in. As Chris pushed the rods down the hole and rattled them about a rabbit shot out of the very first hole we had put Benson in, and shot up the side of the field hedge at about 100mph.

I thought Benson must have bolted the rabbit. Clare and Jed rushed round to the other side of the hedge to see if Benson had come out, but there was still no sign of him. They found a live rabbit caught in one of the nets, though. Chris went and killed the rabbit, then came back. There was still no sign of Benson; it was nearly an hour and half since he had first gone in. Chris gutted the rabbit. I could see Clare was not happy with me for persuading her to put her ferret down a hole. We were discussing what the plan of action would be as the light was starting to dim, when all of a sudden Chris spotted Benson's head poking out of the hole we had put him down. As he went to grab him Benson ran back down the hole.

Grabbing the dead rabbit Chris dangled it into the hole. It wasn't long before Benson sprang out and grabbed hold of the rabbit. As Chris tried to pry Benson off he said, 'It's not your rabbit, I caught it with my drain rods!'

Clare and Jed thought it was Benson who had chased the rabbits out. I didn't care who caught the rabbit. Clare had got Benson back, Chris had got a rabbit, and I could go and get warm.

PANTS ON DOGS

One damp, cold day brother Bob and I were down Roy's place fixing my new car. Bob was replacing the turbo on it. At the time Roy rented his place from a farmer called John. As we were stomping around in the mud and working under the bonnet, John turned up to see what was happening. I noticed he had his dog on a lead. This was unusual as his dogs usually run free.

I made a joke by saying, 'Took up dog walking, John?' 'Huh,' he grunted. 'Dog is on heat and there's a blimmin' dog hangin' round.'

I suggested he caught the dog and took it for a ride. 'I tried that,' said John. 'He bit me when I put him in the Land Rover. I went back later and the bugger had got out!'

Bob perked up from under the bonnet and said, 'You know what you want to do?' 'What?' said John. 'Put a pair of pants on her,' replied Bob. 'A pair of pants?' John sounded surprised. 'Yeah, that's what our uncle did to his dog.'

I thought he was pulling John's leg, as he's very good at winding people up. John asked, 'Will it work?' 'Oh yeah,' said Bob, 'The dog can't get there. Just cut a hole for her tail.' 'Yeah,' said John in agreement.

He'd swallowed the suggestion. Then Bob told him to ask his missus for a pair of old pants, as he would have nothing to lose. 'I'll try it Bob,' John chirped as he walked off.

I never found out if John tried or not, but I could tell from the look on Bob's face that he was just pulling his leg. Pity, because Bob could have taken out a patent on it!

MOTHER NEEDED TO BE REHOUSED

Mother moved back to the yard after Father died and lived there in a caravan for many years. It was her own choice to live back at the family home at Lettaford, where I grew up. The caravans were very old and they were falling to bits. She had hurt her back moving something in the garden and had been taking aspirins. This had given her an ulcer which had caused her to bleed on the inside. I found her on a Wednesday evening when I had gone up to take her shopping, and could see she was not well. Thinking she would refuse to see a doctor I went and fetched her sister Angel to help persuade her to go to hospital.

I decided then that her caravans were not suitable to live in any longer and it was too far for me to go and help her from Exeter.

Peggy's Mum *Photograph courtesy of Peggy Harris*

While she was in hospital having treatment I went to the council to see if I could her on the housing list. I asked what I should do to get my mother rehoused.

The young girl was very helpful and I asked her if she could fill in the forms as I was not a very good speller. So she started to ask questions. 'What's the address? What kind of house does she live in – a flat, a terrace, a bungalow?' 'No,' I said, 'a caravan.' 'A mobile home?' 'No,' I said, 'a 12-foot caravan.' 'How many rooms?' 'Just the one.' 'Toilet?' 'None,' I replied, 'just a bucket.' 'A bucket?' 'There is no running water, or electric. It's her choice.' 'Separate kitchen?' 'None.' 'Bedroom?' 'None.' 'Bathroom?' 'None.' I said no to all her questions. I could see the girl wanted to laugh. I think she thought I was making my mother's case worse than it was, but I wasn't.

She told me I needed to have my mother sign the form and someone from the council would come and visit her to confirm that the answers were correct.

Mother got rehoused in the end by a church charity.

EPILOGUE

About a year ago I had a phone call out of the blue from one of Mother's neighbours saying that they felt she was unwell, since she was asking them to get food for her. Mother never asks for help, so I knew there was something wrong. I arrived on her doorstep at 7am one Monday. She was extremely breathless and the flat was in a real state. I could see that she had several days' worth of part-eaten meals on the table. She was still bristly towards me, and didn't really want me there.

I could see she was in trouble and insisted she needed to go to hospital. I couldn't get her shoes on because her feet were so swollen. I knew it was a heart problem since I'd seen it before, with Roy. Slowly I got her into my car and took her up to the hospital.

While I sat in the waiting room I told her that she needed my help now and that she was to stop pushing me away, and that I would find her all the help I could get. After a short silence she looked up, patted me on the knee, and said, 'I do love you Peg.' I was still feeling defensive and replied, 'Well – it took you 47 years to make up your mind.'

I have been looking for my mother all my life. Now I have found her she is a very sick old lady, with a very bad heart and a cancer lump in her chest. She has only months to live. The nastiness has gone and she has short-term memory loss. She can't think up nasty thoughts about anything or anyone.

She seems to be quite happy, singing and whistling to herself, and wants to sleep a lot. I know she is 88 years old and she has had a long life but I find it hard to watch a very strong-willed and independent woman waste away.

She has carers now who come in, wash and dress her, administer the medication and give her meals four times a day. For three months I had to battle to get her to accept help. I was washing and dressing and cleaning her. It's like she had turned into a giant toddler and I was now mother.

I had trouble with the first carer agency; I found out that they weren't washing her and she became very sore. She wasn't given her medication; it was just left on the side in a bowl. The carer's excuse was that she couldn't get Mother out of her bedroom. The problem was the carer would tell Mother to come to the bathroom then go off and run the water. Mother would forget what the carer had said, and the carer took this as a refusal. She would leave her in her wet nightie, and put her pills on the side. When I came home from work Mother was in a mess. I would ring the agency and complain. The last straw was when a manager came out and gave her breakfast. She'd put salt instead of sugar on her cornflakes and hadn't given Mother her medication. That was it: I changed agency.

I have a few problems with the new agency not recognising Mother's needs for medical assistance, not giving her her meds, turning up late, and so on; but now she has two managers most of the time. They feel that this will give me more confidence, but I can't trust them. The other day I discovered that one of them had overslept and turned up over an hour late!

I feel sorry for elderly people who don't have family to keep an eye on them and monitor the care service. Mother would have died if I hadn't stepped in. I find that when she is OK then I'm fine, but when she is struggling to breathe and I know she is not well it rips me apart inside. It's like I'm grieving for her. I have no control and I'm sorry to say that I have to deal with this mostly on my own. My twin has come round, and my daughter Clare, but the rest of the family don't seem to want to know, or are too old to deal with it. None of them rings me to see how I am, or ask after her, even though I have told them that she is not the nasty woman any more, she's just a frail old woman, it's so sad. Perhaps I should have turned my back on her as she rejected me and shut the door in my face and refused to have anything more to do with me for years.

But I am not like that – after all, she is my Mum.

On the 17th November 2014 Mum sadly passed away in my arms.

ACKNOWLEDGEMENTS

Yet again, without the help of Chris Chapman and his wife Helen, who have spent many hours ploughing through my writings, and giving me advice (and a lot of photographs), this second book would never have been possible. I would also like to thank my daughter Clare for all her help: when I go to visit her she will happily sit for ages typing up my stories.

'Pegs on line' at Throwleigh Fete